THE COMPANY SHE KEEPS
An ethnography of girls' friendship

Valerie Hey

Open University Press
Buckingham • Philadelphia

1 4 667/3

Open University Press
Celtic Court
22 Ballmoor
Buckingham
MK18 1XW

and
1900 Frost Road, Suite 101
Bristol, PA 19007, USA

First Published 1997

A catalogue record of this book is available from the British Library

ISBN   0 335 19406 0 (pb)   0 335 19407 9 (hb)

Library of Congress Cataloging-in-Publication Data
Hey, Valerie.
    The company she keeps : an ethnography of girls' friendship
    /Valerie Hey.
        p.   cm.
    Includes bibliographical references and index.
    ISBN 0–335–19407–9 (hardback). — ISBN 0–335–19406–0 (pbk.)
    1. Teenage girls—Social networks—Great Britain. 2. Girls—
Social networks—Great Britain. 3. Friendship in adolescence—
Great Britain. 4. Interpersonal relations in adolescence—Great
Britain. I. Title.
HQ798.H49   1996
305.23'5'08352—dc20   96–22706
                                                              CIP

Typeset by Graphicraft Typesetters Ltd., Hong Kong
Printed in Great Britain by St Edmundsbury Press Ltd,
Bury St Edmunds, Suffolk

CONTENTS

ACKNOWLEDGEMENTS

In the past year I have been taken by an abiding irony. It concerns the social process of how this book came to be written – namely that in writing a book about the making of femininities I have inadvertently but necessarily been involved in transforming myself into that well-known masculine stereotype: the workaholic. I have had to work unsocial hours: evenings, weekends and during holidays. I have juggled time from multiple projects which were generated on the soft-going of short term contract research and stolen time from the even more intransigent surfaces of family and household life. In the past months I variously recollect: revising chapters on beaches whilst my two daughters splashed in the sea; correcting some text in the company of friends I had invited round for a meal; typing on trains; reading relevant literature on buses, tubes and planes. The project has invariably accompanied me mentally, if not physically, on holiday in Spain and France and in the less exotic locations of Blackpool, Lancaster and Bath – and on the Northern Line and going in and out of Waterloo!

This manuscript thus represents a much travelled and much invested account. Originally in the form of a doctorate written up in what now seems to me, looking back, blissfully empty times – before my children were born and prior to the 'speed up' in academia.

The fact that it has emerged at all owes a great deal to the original and abiding encouragement of Guido Casale; to the cooperation of the girls who were the subjects of the study; to the support of their female teachers who persisted in offering access to allow me to complete the field work; to my supervisors at the University of Kent, Mary Evans and Jeffrey Weeks; and to the personal and intellectual support which has been offered to me by colleagues at my current institution: Jane Miller who read and commented upon Chapters 1, 2 and 8; Jane Kenway who read an early version of the concluding chapter; Diana Leonard who commented incisively on an early paper which formed the basis for the analysis in Chapters 1 and 5; Debbie Epstein; Elaine Unterhalter; Chris Richards; Anne Turvey; Alison Kirton; Melanie Mauthner; Janet Holland and Gemma Moss for their various and generous interest in my work. Janet Maybin's early advice has been invaluable. Additionally Ann Oakley provided insightful editing of an early paper. Recognition is also due to the ESRC who provided financial assistance to support my doctoral study and to the Institute of Education where the Research Board provided a small grant to assist with editing and manuscript preparation, whilst the Staff Development Fund supported my presence at a pertinent conference. In these latter respects Caroline Gipps and Eileen Carnell have sympathetically responded to my requests for financial help. I am also indebted to Jackie Lee, who typed the manuscript, for her patience and skill, and Desna Roberts for help with technical computing advice.

But finally and of most personal significance I want to return to my two beloved daughters and to say thank you to them for understanding my need to get this project out into the public world – and that they will think, at the very least, that their mother was well-occupied as they were busy growing themselves up during the months between January–December 1995. So it is to honour their tolerance of my 'absence' that I dedicate this book to them.

FOREWORD

Ann Oakley

All relationships between women pose something of a threat to a culture like ours, which is organized around the notion that the most important people are men. Male bonding, whether expressed in the physical drama of the football field, the solidarity of masculine talk in the pub, or the masonic dealings that occur in the higher echelons of certain professions, usually passes without comment as a taken-for-granted part of the social fabric. The tradition of heterosexuality incites women to form their main alliances with men. A woman joined to a man is safe. Women's solidarity with one another, on the other hand, is a Pandora's box. What secrets might or do women tell one another? What stories about men and families might they share? What other, coarser, versions of womanhood might be shaped in such narratives?

This wonderfully refreshing book gives us a window on all these themes through the eyes of girls at school, who experience in their real relations with one another a domain of subterfuge, rebellion, power and *pleasure* which in important senses countermands the official lessons of both their schooling and their socialization more generally. As Valerie Hey and others have noted, schools are much more than a vehicle for narrow educational instruction; they also teach boys and girls how to become men and women in a sexist, classist and racist society. But the sociology of schooling has persistently ignored the extent to which messages are also given about emotions and personal relations, those very dimensions of social life in which women are taught to specialize. The making of oneself as a girl is thus not an easy thing, but an activity fraught with all sorts of ambivalences and contradictions.

The Company She Keeps is based on an ethnographic study carried out in two London comprehensive schools in the 1980s. This was a particularly difficult study to do, because the fieldwork demanded access to

places – the subterranean world of girls' friendships – which are precisely designed to keep intruders out. One can speculate on the reasons
why girls' friendships are so exclusionary. Perhaps there's a link with the
peculiar nature of the mother-daughter bond in the gender-differenti-
ated nuclear family? As others have shown, this primary relationship
has a lot to answer for in the whole fascinating business of why women
are disposed to mother and to care for others, while men want to be
cared for, and in their ideas about fathering tend towards a rather different version of parenthood from the one most women hold.

Valerie Hey's account of how research is done in the real world joins
others in demythologizing the mechanistic masculinist model of the social
science textbooks. As is so often the case in real world research, one of
the major resources of the study – the notes girls write to each other 'on
the margins' both literally and metaphorically – emerged by accident as
the research progressed. These scraps of paper, 'illegitimate knowledges',
portray a world of girls' concerns with one another that contrasts with
the boy-centredness of the normative story. In it girls appear in a quite
different guise from the fragmented female subjects of the cultural studies'
accounts. As the girls in their notes hop in and out of the only two
sexual identities expected of them – heterosexual and lesbian – they
succeed in creating an alternative version, one in which women can put
each other first without at the same time constituting themselves as
objects of a sexualized gaze.

Significantly, the teachers in Valerie Hey's study, like society in general
tend to ignore this palpable evidence of girls' friendships unless forced
to confront it when passionate squabbles break out. Then words like
'bitches' and 'witches' are invoked to describe the status of girls' dealings
with one another. Here *The Company She Keeps* indisputably helps to fill
in the female underside of youth culture. Most studies of young people
have focussed on young men and the public evidence of teenage boys'
all too often antisocial solidarity, ignoring whatever it is that young
women, mostly in private, say and do.

While it's well recognized that men and women 'do friendship' differently, we don't understand very much about how, in fact, friendship 'is
done'. Friendship is the least studied of all relationships, despite the fact
that all sorts of studies show that friendship is a very important deter-
minant of health and wellbeing. People who have friends are healthier,
feel better and live longer than those who don't. Social scientists have
largely ignored friendship, reflecting the cultural bias in their preoccupation with the study of male–female relationships, particularly marriage, assuming that these are far more significant and interesting. For
this reason *The Company She Keeps* makes an important contribution to
the sociological literature. It also joins a significant literature which is
concerned with what it's really like to be made (rather than born) a

woman. Locating and describing the cultural expression of this experience involves a highly dedicated archeology: one must above all *listen*;
and one must study the 'problematic' of *everyday life*. Once this is done,
it becomes clear how girls' talk is paralleled by 'womens' talk', by the
ways in which women tell stories to, and about, themselves and one
another. Such 'gossip' may be culturally derogated, but as anthropolo-
gists discovered long ago, it's an invaluable way to learn about a culture.

Above all, perhaps, this book demonstrates yet again that how people
actually experience their lives is much more interesting than how they're
supposed to experience them. For girls and women, the primary task is
to reconcile the expectation and the reality. *The Company She Keeps* shows
how inventive and extraordinary this task really is.

Ann Oakley

Chapter 1

'GRANDIOSE REVELATIONS OF THE OBVIOUS': THEMES OF GIRLS' FRIENDSHIPS

The fish is the last to notice the water.

(Chinese proverb)

Introduction

During the course of my field work I collected the following 'exotic' note:[1]

> Bernice if you must know I don't like you. And I know what you are going to do tomorrow tell your sis.
>
> No, I am not going to tell my sis of you. Marcia's started again (not really) Bernice.
>
> Oh yeh I bet you are. If you feel like being moody go ahead.
>
> I like you, you are being childish.

However, the pacification fails and the second writer joins the first in mutual insults as the text disintegrates into a slanging match:

> You are a little girl who follows shit stirrers.
>
> No that's not true. You must be a s.s.
>
> What's an s.s?
>
> Bloody hell s.s. = shit stirrer.
>
> Dopey Dur!
>
> I know you are.
>
> Well your language is. Well your language isn't very clear. SSABB. And if you don't know what that is well . . .
>
> So what I don't have to know what it means do I?
>
> Well I had to know what s.s. is didn't I? Well its silly slag and boffin breath.

Here represented in their most condensed and dramatic form are some of the themes of this book – issues of girls' intimacy, secrecy and struggle. Early on in her primary school, Jude (one of the subjects of this study) remembers sending a note to another girl: 'Will you be my friend? Tick in the box yes or no'.[2]

Memories of girls' friendship exists as feminine subordinated 'tacit knowledges' (Johnson 1986; Corrigan 1987). This knowledge is often and surprisingly reactivated if we are the mothers of daughters. We are then made only too aware that girls are intensely preoccupied by the micropolitics of their girlfriends, as they insist on 'sleep overs' or worry alternately about invitations or exclusions.

Re/covering memories can provide (possible) confirming evidence of our own girlhoods. Reasons for the cultural suppression of school girl cultures are complex.[3] There is for example, immense ideological pressure to restrict interpretations of these memories. Common sense claims these intricate relations as 'merely a phase' – as a demonstration of a 'natural' feminine capacity for 'caring'. Nostalgia combined with ideologies invested in denying the dangerous notion of complicitous feminine aggression may account for the ways in which we can slide over the violence and passion we might have felt as each others' girlfriends (Wolpe 1988).

Charlotte Brunsdon (1978) has noted the persistence of the view that 'by nature women are inclined to be rather personal'.[4] Certainly the social fact of girls' unique attachments to each other has often been naturalized. One significant consequence has been the minimum recognition of the 'social' within girls' personal forms. The ethnography which follows, in returning us to the terrain of loss and recollection – of girls' pleasure and pain in their friendship – asserts the claims of the social through identifying how it is variously written into the cultural forms of girls' relations with each other.

Marshall Colman criticizes the validity of the enterprise: 'Sociologists have tried to write books about friendship, but what grandiose revelations of the obvious they are!' His preference is for literary accounts that 'reach the heights' (Colman 1982:32) since the peculiarities of the personal are incapable of theorization. Containing the personal within the literary expresses the common anxiety that the issues which the personal encrypts; feelings, emotions, subjectivity, desire and experience disrupt claims to analytic and political rigour. Annette Kuhn (1995) offers a fascinating take upon these important concerns. In puzzling through her co-reliance upon forms of memory and analysis, she argues that if we hold them in creative tension both knowledges can contribute to social and cultural theorizing:

Emotion and memory bring into play a category with which film theory – and cultural theory more generally – are ill equipped to deal;

experience. Indeed they have been wary of making any attempt to tackle it, and quite rightly so. For experience is not infrequently played as the trump card of authenticity, the last word of personal truth, forestalling all further discussion, let alone analysis. Nevertheless, experience is undeniably a key category of everyday knowledge, structuring people's lives in important ways. So, just as I know perfectly well that the whole idea is a fiction and a lure, part of me also 'knows' that my experience – my memories, my feelings – are important because these things make me what I am, make me different from everyone else. Must they be consigned to a compartment separate from the part of me that thinks and analyses? Can the idea of experience not be taken on board – if with a degree of caution – by cultural theory, rather than being simply evaded or worse, consigned to the domain of sentimentality and nostalgia?

(Kuhn 1995:28)

In refusing to abandon the category of 'experience' Kuhn reminds us of the need to hold onto the provocative but troubling everyday knowledges which are, despite their individual mode (in the form of feelings, subjectivities, emotions, memories) intimately related to dominant and systematic features of social life. In locating my analysis in this unsettling territory I too stake a claim to a *sociological* exploration of how every day 'obvious' experience is played out as forms of subjectivity and power. Mischievously I begin through taking a literary turn.

In Margaret Atwood's novel *Cat's Eye*, we are invited into the world where the relationship between memory and culture is incessantly evoked through the narrator's own return to her girlhood world:

Grace is waiting there and Carol, and especially Cordelia. Once I'm outside the house there is no getting away from them. They are on the school bus, where Cordelia stands close beside me and whispers into my ear: 'Stand up straight! People are looking!' Carol is in my classroom, and it's her job to report to Cordelia what I do and say all day. They're there at recess, and in the cellar at lunch time. They comment on the kind of lunch I have, how I hold my sandwich, how I chew. On the way home from school I have to walk in front of them, or behind. In front is worse because they talk about how I'm walking, how I look from behind. 'Don't hunch over,' says Cordelia. 'Don't move your arms like that.' They don't say any of the things they say to me in front of others, even other children: whatever is going on is going on in secret, among the four of us only. Secrecy is important, I know that: to violate it would be the greatest, the irreparable sin. If I tell I will be cast out forever.

But Cordelia doesn't do these things or have this power over me

because she's my enemy. Far from it, I know about enemies. There
are enemies in the schoolyard, they yell things at one another and
if they're boys they fight. In the war there were enemies. Our boys
and the boys from Our Lady of Perpetual Help are enemies. You
throw snowballs at enemies and rejoice if they get hit. With enemies you can feel hatred, and anger. But Cordelia is my friend. She
likes me, she wants to help me, they all do. They are all my friends,
my girlfriends, my best friends. I have never had any before and I'm
terrified of losing them. I want to please.

(Atwood 1990:119–20)

In Atwood's novel, the narrator, Elaine Risley, plots her memories of
girlhood in intense episodes such as the one above. The heroine eventually and (thankfully) triumphs over the tyrannical Cordelia, but not
before we are invited to participate in a detailed literary psychosocial
drama through which we trace what is at stake in girls' embodied relations with each other. The novel takes as its central theme one that involves us here – an interrogation of those myriad interstices of feminine
power which are forms of girls' giving (and withholding) of friendship.
The fictive 'policing' episode above dramatizes the same modality of
power which was shown in the form and content of the girls' note. This
specific modality of intimate power runs as an abiding theme in later
chapters. If sociologists are poor substitutes for novelists, it would appear
that novelists are capable of substantial ethnographic insight.[5]

We are for example, made aware of the collective and hence cultural
enterprise set in motion through Cordelia's apparent 'whims'. We can
see confirmed the importance of the 'private', the secret and the 'invisible' as giving a peculiarly intense inflexion to the bonds of domination
and subordination. We are also given a glimpse into how Elaine's subjecthood as an embodied being is established as *the* site to be inspected
in intimate detail ('They comment on how I hold my sandwich, how I
chew'). We note the consequences of Elaine's humiliation and suffering
in the forms of her own embodied self-mutilation (peeling the skin from
her feet).

The overwhelming impression is of a subjecthood lived against unwrit-
ten rules and unvoiced notions of her friends definition of 'normality'.
Elaine remarks that 'I am just not measuring up, although they are giving
me every chance. I will have to do better. But better at what?'

Locked out from the explicit in this isolating gendered and embodied
time and space path (Giddens 1985), Elaine like Saskia in this study (or
Princess and Sally) are frequently (and sometimes permanently) placed
on the margins of their respective groups through the axis of difference
('I am not normal, I am not like other girls'; Atwood 1990:118). For me,
as for Tuula Gordon, marginality is an analytic category (Gordon 1995).

It speaks to adhesions between social and cultural power and refers to 'multiple social axes intertwined in relations of structural and cultural power. Thus marginality does not signify powerlessness in any simple sense' (Gordon 1995:7).[6]

The following analysis reads girl–girl relations as located 'in the margins', in the clandestine, the obscure and the shifting instances of friendships' social formation and dissolution as their key defining moments (Side 1995).

Locating margins: common sense constructions

From my study it emerged that, for girls, 'being rather personal' was treated with indifference except when girls' absorption with each other erupted into passionate fallouts. Then girls were viewed as 'dangerous'. I have heard staff criticize girls as 'bitches' or 'witches'. The following passage from another study captures the sense of unease:

> Parents and teachers continually acknowledge the importance and influence that a child's peers have in their orientation to and interpretation of school experience. A teacher in the school where this research was conducted illustrates this point when he is talking about a girl with whom he is spending a considerable time counselling. 'I'm convinced it's not her, though, *it's the company she keeps,* particularly that—Do you remember her? That's where the trouble lies.'
>
> (Meyenn 1980:108, emphasis added)

Other research has understood girls' 'conformity' as part of the social compliance demanded by a specific ethical cultural code (Nilan 1991; Griffiths 1995). Paradoxically girls' affiliations *do* offer a rationale for the tendency to treat girls as less individualized than boys, since girls have a vested interest in reproducing themselves as mirroring their friends. This provides the material base for the well-known phenomenon of girls' general invisibility in teacher recall. A deputy head at one of my research sites (Eastford School) held another common stigmatizing view: 'You were more likely to find boys who were either brilliant or duffers, than girls who are more like each other' (field notes, Eastford School).

There are some compelling paradoxes in all of this – an intensity of girls' emotional and social investments in each other on the one hand – indifference or diagnosed pathology and a lack of sociological interest on the other. This book investigates why these relations continue to matter so much to schoolgirls. After all, in such a hostile climate we should be especially curious about girls' persistent investments in each other.

Metaphors and mis/understandings: readings in schoolgirls and culture

If we turn to academic as opposed to vernacular 'common sense' accounts, we discover that whilst they pay girls different sorts of attention, they seldom pay them the amount of attention they pay each other. In short, girls' same-sex relationships have been variously overlooked, over-romanticized, overpoliticized and oversimplified. The remainder of this chapter explores how girls in groups have been previously conceptualized in some cognate fields.[7] The following critical review examines the accumulation of metaphors developed by various theoretical languages.

Translating subjects into theoretical terms is always a metaphorical process constructing some parts of experience into something else. But if 'metaphors can draw attention to unexpected aspects of social phenomena', they can also 'inevitably obscure or hide other aspects from view' (Davis 1994:360). However something more fundamental occurs in the literature about girls. In the process of being translated into male dominated theories, empirical girls almost disappear.[8]

'The implications of the implications of confusion'[9]

Mandy Llewellyn's neglected and tantalizing article summarizes the difficulties involved in 'studying girls at school':

> How could I understand their relations with each other, with their teachers, the relationship of school-based activities and behaviour to the wider social context of estate life, suburbia and the home and family setting? Partly this is explained by the complexity of social reality. But more importantly I would argue that it was because I was unconsciously trying to understand what was going on around me in relation to existing concepts and frameworks of analysis, whilst not recognising or questioning the limitations due to what they were based upon: empirical work on boys at school and male youth culture, and a neglect of gender as a sociologically significant dimension of analysis.
>
> (Llewellyn 1980:44–5)

The difficulty is even more deep-seated than Llewellyn recognized. It is not 'merely' that feminine experience is excised in youth culture and the ethnographic analytic accounts which tried to capture its popular forms, but more problematically the theory of culture which underpins 'youth culture' is proposed as universal, whilst being in effect, a highly gendered account. Endeavouring to insert girls into cultural accounts thus leaves the problem of the gendered nature of culture unproblematized and masculinist presumptions untouched.

The following discussion explores a further range of metaphorical discourses about girls before returning to considerations of what would be required to reinvent a feminist theorization of culture which *could* accommodate girls. First, I look briefly at symbolic interactionism followed by radical feminist classroom observation studies before moving on briefly to gloss the social psychological literature. At this point I consider in more detail the influential feminist intervention represented by the Harvard Project (Gilligan *et al.* 1990; Brown and Gilligan 1992). I turn next to other related material, namely the philosophy inspired work which also reads girls' friendship through a moral dimension. I end the review with a critical examination of the subcultural framing of social experience.

'Girls with attitude': studying girls at school and theorizing interactions

The symbolic–interactionist literature provided many memorable images of girls; however their purpose was to illustrate aspects of the institution of schooling rather than girls' own cultures (Furlong 1976; Lambart 1976; Meyenn 1980; Pollard 1984). When girls' intergroup behaviours *were* studied, similarities in intragroup structures and processes were overlooked (Meyenn 1980). Girls were read primarily in terms of their different school *attitudes*. Prior questions about how such attitudes were socially plotted *within* a group remain obscured. The writers did not search for explanations in terms of significant gender, class or race dimensions – the object of our gaze is that 'strange, ungendered isolate "The Child"' (Ennew 1994:127):

> Carol, Valerie, Diana, Jill, Debbie, Anne, Angela and Monica are sitting close together. Debbie is playing with one of Carol's shoes; Valerie and Diana are reading comics and Carol is combing her hair and occasionally making jokes quietly to those around her. By and large no-one in the class seems very interested in the content of the lesson . . . eventually the teacher 'notices' that Valerie and Diana are reading comics and demands to have them. Diana quietly gives hers up but Valerie says 'Oh no sir, *please* don't take it'. The teacher insists and takes it away until lunchtime. Carol immediately gets out another magazine from her bag, turns round to Valerie and Diana and they all start looking at it.
>
> (Furlong 1976:39)

This scenario is constructed as a 'definition of a non-learning situation' (Furlong 1976). It is also simultaneously depoliticized and indeed desocialized. Corrigan puts it well:

My main critique of those who see social interactional practices producing and reproducing societies is that they displace or condense
(or both) the content and the form of the repertoires through which
we handle, name, structure and make those social relations because
we are coerced or encouraged to do so if we want to be recognised,
understood, heard, seen and so on. The understanding of the construction of the regulation of repertoires is what is so crucial, to understand how the archaeology of schooling is alive, in its, that is to say,
our, present.

(Corrigan 1987:38–9 note 39)

Any severance of girls' cultural practices from considerations of power
leaves us no way to think about girls as social agents except in terms of
the apparently *ad hoc* reactions of individual girls to individual teachers.
This is not a fate that awaits girls' groups theorized by feminists working within the subcultural tradition. Here identical practices are read as
an expression of a 'class based instinct' the perpetrators (white working-
class girls) are said to invest in a form of 'hyper femininity' subversive
of both bourgeois 'niceness' and academic success:

Thus the girls took great pleasure in wearing makeup to school,
spent vast amounts of time discussing boyfriends in loud voices in
class and used these interests to disrupt the class. In answer to the
question, how do you spend your time during the maths lesson,
two girls replied:

Sue: Carve names on me desk, anything that comes into my head
        – boys' names, Woody, Eric, Les. Then when I've done that
        I start writing on me plimsolls.

Karen: Comb me hair under the lid of the desk, put on me makeup,
        look in the mirror.

(McRobbie 1978:104)

Here McRobbie's emphasis on the visual is characteristic of the subcultural compulsion to read style as politics. It is not that either readings are
without insight – it is just that we get only a restricted sense of the complex relays between the micro and the macro in both accounts. Whilst
the former bleaches girls of their gender, the second privileges an interpretation in which femininity is rendered as inescapably a function of
capital relations. McRobbie herself has argued subsequently for an account
which, whilst clearly recognizing the salience of class, would be much
more pliable:

At the same time I did tend to pull in class wherever I could in this
study ['Working class girls and the culture of femininity'] often when
it simply wasn't relevant. Perhaps I was just operating with an inade-
quate notion of class, but there certainly was a disparity between my

'wheedling in' class in my report and its complete absence from the girls' talk and general discourse . . . Being working class meant little or nothing to these girls – but being a *girl* over determined their every moment . . . [Now she would investigate] how relations of power and powerlessness permeated the girls' lives – in the context of school, authority, language, job opportunities, the family, the community and sexuality.

(McRobbie 1982b:48)

Boys on top, girls in silence: radical feminist classroom observation studies

The radical feminist approach (Spender and Sarah 1980; Stanworth 1981; Mahony 1985) demonstrates different theoretical inflexibilities. For example, the writers are also transfixed by the relationships between teachers and their pupils and the nature of classroom interactions. However, unlike the mainstream symbolic interactionist literature, which manages to overlook gender (see Wolpe 1988), writers like Stanworth (1981), Mahony (1985) and Spender and Sarah (1980) make it their business to focus upon the structuring effects of gender through theorizing the impact of boys' behaviour. Boys are said to dominate teacher time, classroom space and girls. We learn little about girls' relations with each other. Girls tend to be presented through the lens of their male tormentors as 'the faceless bunch' (Stanworth 1981:39). Girls' invisibility and assumed academic underachievement is read as proof of patriarchy and boys' verbal and physical violence is seen to be its defining moment. The limitation of this approach is that it relies upon stereotypes of 'typical' boys as limiting and banal as those which feminists have critiqued when applied to girls. Not all boys are Neanderthal man, nor all girls passive victims. Notions of heterogeneity imported through the important dimensions of class, ethnicity, race, age and sexuality considerably complicate our readings of 'girls' and 'boys' (Jones 1988, 1993). The absence of 'differences' tends to restrict our understandings and dilute our appreciation of the multiple sources of power within which school subjects live their histories.

Social psychology constructs the friend

The most systematic studies of friendship have been informed by social psychology (Rubin 1980; Asher and Gottman 1981; Epstein and Karweit 1983; Smilansky 1991). Psychological studies confirm the intense interest children have in socializing with each other as well as the tendency for groups to be segregated by gender (Lever 1976; Rubin 1980; Corsaro

1984). There is a consensus that feminine and masculine subjects 'do friendship' differently (O'Connor 1992).[10]

Social psychology however, whilst it has a great deal to say about friendship, has little to offer researchers who are trying to link the interpersonal with the social. The discipline's traditional domination by an individualist framing of 'development' makes it difficult to ask the sort of questions which concern us here. The nearest we get to the 'social' is through the notion of popularity. One consequence of the framework is that gender becomes one of many variables. Evident differences between female and male friendship are then 'explained' through essentialist notions of masculinity or femininity: 'A boy needs a group. He wants a gang of rebels with whom he can identify and to gain the strength he needs for a stance against adult authority' (Douvan and Adelson 1966:201–2).

Apart from the audacity of this particular version of the myth of heroic male bonding, one is struck by the reading of male friendship as an avowedly public orientation. The literature on feminine friendship by contrast emphasizes its essentially private and intimate nature (Johnson and Aries 1983a, 1983b; O'Connor 1992).

Some recent attempts in the United States (Bush and Simmons 1987; Simmons and Blyth 1987; Gilligan *et al.* 1990) have tried to break out of the developmental tradition through an analytic focus on grounding aspects of adolescent girls' psychological self-concepts in the social. For example, Simmons and Blyth (1987:95) identify the particular combination of girls' generally higher investment in 'looks' with their overall lower self-esteem. Intriguingly, the authors develop Hill and Lynch's (1983) Gender-Intensification Hypothesis in the direction of suggesting that the splitting of identity into gender binaries is secured in gendered locations. Whilst masculinity is associated with the prestigious public sphere, femininity emerges much more strongly identified and (penalized) through its association with the socially denigrated private sphere. This in itself adds to the difficulties girls have in managing their growth into adolescence. The sociological resonances of this psychosocial hypothesis has already been indicated and will be displayed in more detail in the ensuing data chapters.

Girls on top: moral correctness and the feminine realm

One highly influential formulation of the relationship between girls and schooling has been the social–psychological 'discovery' of girls as moral agents (Gilligan 1982; Gilligan *et al.* 1990; Brown and Gilligan 1992). Space does not allow a systematic appreciation of this large body of interesting and insightful work. I concentrate here upon the work into girls' schooling (Gilligan *et al.* 1990; Brown and Gilligan 1992). There has been a detailed discussion of this work elsewhere (see Segal 1987; Stacey 1990; Haste 1993; *Feminism and Psychology* 1994). I wish to make only a couple of points about the representation of girls in *Meeting at the Crossroads* (Brown and Gilligan 1992).[11]

From the outset it is important to acknowledge the sense of relief one experiences in discovering that there is at least one account which tries to originate a theoretical account from 'listening to girls'. I certainly had a strong initial desire to confirm the general truth of the Brown and Gilligan proposition – that of girls' social development told through the metaphor of voice – of the confident voice of girlhood replaced by the diminished and un/voiced self of adolescence. Certainly the idea of 'losing voice' does capture in common idiom the feeling that we, as women, are always pleasing others rather than ourselves.

However my own data were more ambiguous, representing fragmented and contradictory feminine subjects with contextually variant assertive as well as diminished voices – findings which were impossible to reconcile with the conceptualization of the 'Harvard' authentic self-validating girl subject. There was also resistance in the shape of my discomfort with the images and claims about women in authority, despite the overall seductiveness of the 'voice' approach. For example, the following 'analytic' and apocalyptic moment trades in the discourse of maternal guilt-induction, namely 'bad mothers' versus 'good mothers':

> It was first with a sense of shock and then a deep, knowing sadness that we listened to the voices of the girls tell us that it was the adult women in their lives that provided the models for silencing themselves and behaving like 'good little girls'. We wept. Then the adult women in our collective girlhoods came into the room. We could recall the controlling, silencing women with clarity and rage, but we could also gratefully recall the women who had allowed our disagreement and rambunctiousness in their presence and who had made us feel whole.
>
> (Pat, a member of the school administration quoted in Brown and Gilligan 1992:221)

Or this extract with its peculiarly unreflexive racist imagery that echoes back to the Conrad (1960) of *The Heart of Darkness*, rather than forward to sustained critical commentary:

> Meeting at this crossroads creates an opportunity for women to join girls and by doing so to reclaim lost voices and lost strengths, to strengthen girls' voices and girls' courage as they enter adolescence by offering girls resonant relationships, and in this way to move with girls toward creating a psychologically healthier world and a more caring and just society. In providing this account of our meeting with a particular group of girls and describing the relationships

that developed between girls and women, we report a way into what has been a dark continent in women's development – a crisis of relationship which has been covered over by lies. The horror, psychologically speaking which is at the centre of this crisis is the realization that girls are not only enacting dissociation but also narrating the process of their own disconnection – revealing its mechanisms and also its intention. The girls in our study, as they approached adolescence, were finding themselves at a relational impasse; in response, they were sometimes making, sometimes resisting a series of disconnections that seem at once adaptive and psychologically wounding; between psyche and body; voice and desire, thoughts and feelings, self and relationship. The central paradox we will explore – the giving up of relationship for the sake of 'Relationships' – is a paradox of which girls themselves are aware.

(Brown and Gilligan 1992:6–7)

Theorists like Walkerdine (1987), Alcoff (1988), Davies (1989), Walkerdine and Lucey (1989) and Jones (1993) have preferred to analyse subjectivity in terms of the effects of competing, irreconcilable and contradictory discourses. Identity is thus always understood as an incompletion – a struggle and a process (Hall 1990). Walkerdine (1987) has used the metaphor of performance and drawn upon the notion of masquerade (Riviere 1985). Kathy Davis puts it well when she argues:

Imagine if you will, that femininity is fragmented, messy or haphazard rather than coherent and authentic. Or that the expression of identity is a contingent and temporary business rather than a matter of finding one's true self. Or that femininity is a kind of ongoing project which has to be ongoingly constructed through social interaction rather than an object to be discovered, suppressed or lost.

(Davis 1994:360)

The Harvard Project's 'authentic' girl is thus (despite assertions to the contrary, see Brown 1994) a profoundly asocial subject. This is connected to how 'she' is produced in the text. The predominant image is a subject, as both a daughter and schoolgirl, invariably locked in gladiatorial combat with mothers, teachers and other girls.

Whilst Brown and Gilligan's work (like that of Valerie Walkerdine's) and this study (importantly and painfully) implicates other feminine subjects in girls oppression, we need more than this, not least because this is complicit with anti-feminism.[12] Jane Miller argues (after applauding Walkerdine's work of demythologizing child-centred pedagogies), that what is required are more analytical narratives which, having identified 'the bullying, the coercion, even the violence to be found . . . trac[es] the histories which have implicated women so damagingly in these sorts of double binds' (1991:36).

The Harvard Project cannot answer these sorts of questions. This inability is particularly marked in the account of girls' cultures (Brown and Gilligan 1992), where the proffering of individual moral biographies provides little purchase upon the divisions through which girls live their lives with and against each other. The élite nature of the school and the predominance of élite girls over minority or working-class girls would suggest a common sense recognition of the ways in which girls in Emma Willard succeed in doing power over each other. But this recognition is deferred time and time again. A stronger insistence upon accepting the implications of the existence of inequalities between girls would have made it more difficult to read young girlhood as a rite of passage during which their 'voiced' innocence is stolen from them by wicked stepmothers, 'witches' and other denying older females.

As other commentators have noted, girlhood is also a time in which girls come to learn how to take up their place in multiple and competing regimes of power (Ashendon et al. 1987; Mac an Ghaill 1994). Differences of class and race are important social markers (Llewellyn 1980; Mirza 1992; Hey 1994, 1995a, 1995b), whilst taking up positions within heterosexuality confers differing (if troubling) forms of social power associated with girls' different claims upon its prestige (Skeggs 1994; Hey 1994, 1995a, 1995b), whilst the micro-social politics around notions of 'beauty' have been noted (Ashendon et al. 1987; Canaan 1986).

In contrast, Emma Willard's girls are effectively decontextualized from wider and cross-cutting social and material conditions of their lives. This neatly avoids considerations of how feminine 'double binds' stem not only from the power imbalances held between women and girls (in their roles as mothers/daughters–teachers/students) but we have no take upon how power is constructed from the differential social powers held amongst girls themselves. This gives us only a one-dimensional (gendered) intergenerational understanding of subjects' complex investments in silencing and being silenced. Most problematically of all, it offers us no real sense of how the material oppressions of hegemonic forms of masculinity, class and race mediate and distribute differentiated gender effects. Maybe the pursuit of a psychology (as opposed to a sociology) of girls compels the individualizing emphasis, but this does then weaken claims for political and analytical insight (see contributions to *Feminism and Psychology* 1994; especially articles by Lykes and Gremmen).

Re/sisters: philosophical and historical accounts of feminine friendship

There have been other important (philosophical) studies (some influenced by the Harvard Project) focused upon the ethical dimensions of feminine friendship (Faderman 1981; Raymond 1986; White 1990; Nilan 1991). These writers explore the moral themes of women's and girls' friendship groups, though they do this through different disciplinary codes (Side 1995). Nilan, drawing upon the work of Gilligan and her colleagues, implies that girls have a particular commitment to ethically sound relationships:

> My argument in this article is that interactions and friendship networking between girls should not be explained in simplistic and dismissive terms if the aim is to understand the wider cultural practices that inform this networking. I propose that friendship between girls can be explained in part as an accomplishment within a mutually understood moral order. This moral order pertains to caring, trust and loyalty and depends upon girls continually demonstrating to other girls that they can 'do' the moral work of friendship properly. In broad terms, transgressions of the moral order of friendship bring about processes of exclusion.
>
> (Nilan 1991:167)

Using Lynn Davies's (1979) work into the construction of moral ordering, she details the framing of girls inclusionary and exclusionary 'moments' of making and breaking of friendship:

> It seems to me that beginning to look at friendship between girls, not in terms of a pre-determined model of pervasive, yet invisible patriarchal constraints, but in terms of lived moments of interactions between and with girls who are actually going on with the business of being friends in their talk, goes some way towards fulfilling what Dorothy E. Smith (1988) maintains is the first step towards making a sociology from the standpoint of women.
>
> (Nilan 1991:164)

Whilst I find her analysis compelling – the detailed attention to the features of girls' talk is, I think, absolutely salient – I remain unconvinced by her theoretical decision to quarantine the moral and social decision making of girls' friendship from an analysis of the patriarchal social structures of school and community. The empirical evidence of her own study shows the impossibility of segmenting reality – sexual divisions are the terms through which we encounter the social world. There are numerous instances where the burden of keeping out 'the lads' proves too much, for example the references to the 'truth test' imposed by a group of girls upon one girl directly references a strategy of attacking a girl as a 'liar' by inventing some knowledge concerning boys. Equally, the language of punishment directed at those girls who fail the moral tests of friendship draw upon the patriarchal catch-all abusive term for girls and women: 'slut' (see Lees 1986). It is perhaps interesting to note that Prue (one of the girls excluded) confronted her former friends by calling them 'just really slack'![13] The linguistic presence of the pervasive and perverting patriarchal world alerts us to the need to theorize girls' relations with each other as *invariably* structured through the assumptions of heterosociality and heterosexuality (Cockburn 1986).

The consistent tendency to idealize girl–girl relations on the assumption that they are male-free, whilst at the same time providing evidence to the contrary is interesting. Much as we might like the comfort of imagining a realm 'beyond power', 'beyond boys and men', the evidence of the indivisibility of the sexes suggest that we should be wary of accounts which exclude boys and men since they are amongst the conditions of women's and girls' subordination. Boys do not have to be there in actuality to exercise power. They sometimes only need to be there 'in the head' (Holland *et al.* 1991; Rossiter 1994).

'A working class hero is something to be': subcultural theory and 'the lads'

The previous critique has argued that girl-friendly theories have tended to celebrate girls as moral actors and either ignored or insufficiently understood the importance of girls' social differences and so restricted our understandings about what is at stake for girls in their struggles with schooling and within relationships. Ironically, the same romanticized effect arises even if the theory which generated it – subculture or the 'gang of lads' model (Griffin 1995) – is predicated on male behaviour.

Subcultural theory is the most widely used account of the relationships between culture, power and schooling. It is an account dominated by the theoretical legacy of Gramsci (1971). The most ambitious and sustained engagement with his ideas has been within the Centre for Contemporary Cultural Studies, University of Birmingham (CCCS). At issue, in terms of increasing our understandings about girls, are the influential theoretical writings about culture, cultural hegemony and resistance.

Gramsci's notion of hegemony remains central to an understanding of how the cultural is implicated in the maintenance or disruption of forms of power (Hebdige 1979; Hall and Jefferson 1980; Epstein 1993; Mac an Ghaill 1994). It underpins the radical theorization of youth collective forms as counter-hegemonic – it has been argued that youth subcultures were 'symbolic forms of resistance . . . spectacular symptoms of a wider and more generally submerged dissent' (Hebdige 1979:80). There is nothing inherently masculine in the definition of culture which underpinned subcultural ethnographies, 'that level at which social groups developed distinct patterns of life and give *expressive form* to their social and material life-experience' (Hall and Jefferson 1980:10, emphasis in original).

The definition of 'group' and 'expressive forms', however, was operationalized through masculine cultural codes which obscured the fact that, as McRobbie (1980:45) says, 'it's different for girls'. Those public leisure cultures of the streets and the 'lads' were not only less available to girls, girls were also significantly less interested in occupying them.

Empirically underrepresented and theoretically eliminated, girls were relegated to the sidelines of what was in effect a masculine (if not masculinist) version of cultural production and transmission. Other channels, other forms of the creation and distribution of knowledge were ignored. Instead we have as our focus the carnival of costumes in which young men, rendered as sociological and cultural clothes horses await ethnographic deconstruction by male experts (Hebdige 1976, 1979; Clarke 1980).

Dressing the part

It was not accidental therefore that subcultural studies of skinheads, hippies and the mods emphasized the visual differentiations of masculine surfaces and style (Willis 1977; Hebdige 1979; Clarke 1980), since this was the crucial starting (and for some end) point for the ethnographic project:

> The raw material of history could be seen refracted, held and 'handled' in the line of a mod's jacket, in the soles of a teddy boy's shoes. Anxieties concerning class and sexuality, the tension between conformity and deviance, family and school, work and leisure, were all frozen there in a form which was at once visible and opaque.
>
> (Hebdige 1979:78)

If male ethnographers could read cultural history from the soles of a teddy boy's shoes, it is hardly surprising that they were less than interested in talking to them! The obsessive attention to form, literally as well as theoretically, covered from view denser questions about the hidden content – the formations/recreation and negotiation of masculine sexual and social identity which public forms carried. The less visual, interpersonal realm (despite being incessantly invoked) was almost entirely eliminated (Clarke 1982). We never discovered, for example, what happened when the skinhead returned home to change his Ben Sherman, after a hard day out on the street. The private world of home, as well as the more intimate world of boys' heterosocial/heterosexual relationships were silenced, along with the girls and women who inhabited them. What of the sisters, mothers and girlfriends who laboured there so that the 'lads' could strut their stuff outside? What of the desires and pains of male ado-lescence? Where are the masculine insecurities and anxieties (McRobbie 1980; Holland *et al.* 1993)? In editing out the private the writers effect-ively reproduced the oppressive practices which they were compelled to document: 'You didn't need to get too heavily into sex or pulling chicks, or sorts as they were called. *Women were just the people who were dancing over in the corner by the speakers'* (Pete Meaden quoted in McRobbie 1980:43, emphasis added).

As numerous feminist cultural theorists have argued, access to, and use of, public space is itself structured in conditions of difference – whether one is a girl or a woman, black or white, young or old, able-bodied or disabled (Gotfrit 1988; Gordon 1995; Griffin 1995). Most significantly it is girls after all who are frequently objectified and 'consumed' in public spaces:

> Women play a crucial part in men's 'leisure', whether as escorts (paid or unpaid), prostitutes, or simply as objects of the male gaze. (A 35 year old university lecturer recently informed me that he and a colleague frequently spent the evening at a city centre disco; 'We only go to look at the girls').
>
> (Griffin 1982:4)

Becoming a 'spectacular disaffiliate' (Hebdige 1979) was hardly a vi-able option for the majority of boys, the so-called 'normals', 'the earoles' – those who were subsequently consigned to theoretical and political oblivion (see Clarke 1982), let alone for even more marginalized groups. This should have stimulated important questions about the different shapes and contours of girls' specific production of culture and cultural forms (McRobbie and Garber 1980) as well as more substantial empirical investigations.

Subcultural writers however, persisted in shoehorning girls into mod-els derived from observing highly specialized male behaviour. Girls were thus invariably rendered in terms of an achieved subordination to a pat-riarchal order:

> Skinhead girls admire the way their boys treat them *as if they weren't there*. They never include them in their conversation, you must do this yourself, they never introduce you to new friends. They have no manners, are cheeky and disrespectful, but the girls respect them for being this way.
>
> (14-year-old girl quoted in Frith 1981:63–4, emphasis added)

Questions about how the subordinations of gender produced girls as accomplices in these subcultural formations remained.

There have been and continue to be numerous efforts to reposition sub-cultural theory as a way to theorize girls' collective experience. McRobbie

(1980) is possibly the most persuasive and consistent attempt at rehabilitating subculture at the level of theory (see also Cockburn 1987). There are some dissenting voices. Whilst acknowledging the seductive pleasures of style, Elizabeth Wilson drawing upon the work of Walter Benjamin cautions against the 'aesthetisization of politics':

> Even the bizarre can be fashionable and attempts to outrage or (as often happens) to be overtly sexual or sexual in some different way, may nevertheless remain within stylistic boundaries of clothes that still express submissiveness to a boyfriend, even if they spell rebellion at home.
>
> (Wilson 1983:24)

McRobbie herself acknowledged in devastating detail both how highly sex-differentiated 'style' is – 'It's punk girls who wear the suspenders after all!' – and furthermore she notes,

> Women are so obviously inscribed (marginalised, abused) within subcultures as static objects (girl-friends, whores, or 'fag-heaps') that access to its thrills, to hard fast rock music, to drugs, alcohol and 'style' would hardly be compensation for even the most adventurous teenage girl.
>
> (McRobbie 1980:43)

It continues to be an irresistible source of fascination for subcultural commentators, however:

> To the extent that all-girl subcultures, where the commitment to the gang comes first, might forestall these processes and provide their members with a collective confidence which could transcend the need for 'boys', they could well signal an important progression in the politics of youth culture.
>
> (McRobbie 1980:49)

There is an urgent need here to insert the practice of reflexivity. As other commentators have pointed out (including McRobbie herself) subcultural ethnographies bear the additional weight of their (male) authors' desires. Gary Clarke pointedly remarks that the recovery of the working class in subcultural terms completely inverted the Left's earlier position: 'Rather than being seen as a diversion from the "historic destiny" of the working class (or as expressions of "false consciousness") youth subcultures have been seen as *the* expression of the working class in struggle' (Clarke 1982:20).

The imposition of an explanatory model derived from male behaviour thus carries a double irony, since not only do feminist in/appropriations repeat the tendency to position subcultural girls as 'semiotic guerrillas', they also carry traces of feminist desire that girls discontinue their investments in boys and heterosexuality. If there is a standard 'return of the repressed' shared across all of the accounts it is that of a radical longing for a pro-feminist heroine and prefigurative feminist practice.

Here is Richard Johnson (1986:306–7), an important and sympathetic cultural critic reviewing the feminist work on girls: 'Cultural forms are also related to an analysis of social relations . . . feminist work on girl culture for instance, has been as preoccupied with theorising *women's position* as with talking to girls' (emphasis added). It is not that I dissent from his understanding of what is at stake here, nor from what the feminist accounts *have* focused upon. It is more that he repeats rather than interrogates 'the sins of the mothers' in collapsing the specificities of girls (yet again) into adult modes of femininity. Talking to girls does not apparently guarantee that they will have their 'own' theory sensitive to the specific material condition of girlhoods (see Miller 1991 on McRobbie).

If we were to problematize the process through which the 'public' facts of girls as each others' friends is complexly and contradictorily converted into different 'truths' about girls (and of our selves), we might begin to understand how the workings of power/knowledge (Foucault 1980) se-cure the meanings of girls and girls' cultures in terms which systematic-ally and adamantly refuse to acknowledge the passionate and systematic attachments schoolgirls have to their female friends.

Chris Griffin (1995) notes that the phenomenon of collective forget-ting is common in female culture, creating barriers across female genera-tions and between heterosexual and lesbian girls and women. Ros Coward suggests one of the reasons for our collective forgetting is the dearth of public cultural forms within which we can reclaim the specific cultural experiences of feminine friendships: 'The problem is not just that women don't see the centrality they have for each other reflected anywhere . . . it's also that feminism has leapt in to fill the gap with a somewhat idealised notion of friendship' (Coward 1986:).[14]

It is, as Coward implies, important to locate the specific practices of girls' friendship cultures on different grounds than feminine essentialism (i.e. of femininity as 'nurturance' or even rebellion). Such treacherously seductive images are substantially disconfirmed in the following ethno-graphy. What follows is a far more ambivalent account of girls located in economies of friendships as sites of power *and* powerlessness. The next chapter establishes different grounds for studying girls and different ways into the 'confusions'.

Notes

1 The note was handed to me at Crossfield School. A teacher had discovered it after one of her lessons.

2 Another colleague has remarked how girls' informal literacies mimic the official writing and pedagogic practices of school – namely multiple choice. See the other samples of ethnographic data in the chapters to follow. I am indebted to Anne Gold for this perception.

3 Every time I have given a presentation of my work on girls' friendships the response from the female audience is akin to that of rediscovering a forgotten world. A 'rush of nostalgia' is how one participant described it. I prefer the less euphoric term of 'collective forgetting' to capture the ideological effort which has sustained this excision of the importance of our girlfriends (see Smith-Rosenberg 1975; Raymond 1986; Griffin 1995).

4 She cites the judge who further remarked that: 'They attach themselves to persons. They become fond of people and they are inclined to follow them, and they may follow them to their detriment because they are fond of them' (Brunsdon 1978:18). I recognize that citing judges is the sociological equivalent of taking sweets off babies but the implicit comparison of women to dogs is startling and it nicely dramatizes the prevalent social ideology of femininity as simultaneously caring and dependent.

5 Episodes like the one cited are so consonant with both the more negative memories of my own girlhood as well as my data that I am completely convinced by the power of imagining and memory as sources of social and cultural comment. Interestingly I deliberately did *not* read Atwood until I had finished the main draft of the book, in case it 'contaminated' my interpretation! I can only imagine that despite my intellectual commitment to the notion of situated readings, part of me was at some level invested in the unsustainable notion of a 'pure reading'.

6 Additionally it is crucial to retain something of the meaning of margins as a metaphor of space and limitation (as well as opportunity) – to understand how girls do occupy and take up their embodied gendered space at school. Gotfrit's work on the struggles to take up space on the dance floor is a reminder that space is physical and policed by the powerful. Her deliberate and subversive decision to 'dance back' into the public space of the dance floor is specifically contrasted with the practices of other women and girls who 'spent large parts of their evening in the women's washroom in order to be together' (Gotfrit 1988:133). I also want to capture the sense of girls as discursively productive in the 'margins' – that they are, if you like, engaged in making 'really useful' (gendered) knowledge.

7 I have been both partial in the choice, as well as polemical in the discussion of the literatures. For those wanting a more temperate discussion, O'Connor (1992) is good on the literature on women's friendships, whilst Griffiths (1995) includes references to current research in an accessible and helpful way. There are therefore many other points of entry into the subject – but since I wanted to map the overlapping domains of schooling, collective and cultural meanings and social practices, I went to the dominant radical paradigm first. I consider the intellectual legacy of the literature on culture and subcultures still reverberating in the new feminist rewriting of female friendship as related myths intent on the glamorization of another group of the disenfranchised.

8 Wittig's attack on the status of women in Lévi-Strauss's structuralist account

of kinship identifies what could be termed a metaphorical tendency in male theoretical writing: 'Has he not indeed written of women? He writes that you are currency, an item of exchange. He writes barter, barter, possession and acquisition of women and merchandise. Better for you to see your guts in the sun and utter the death rattle than to live a life that anyone can appropriate' (Wittig 1973:115–16).

9 I am taking some liberties with the subtitle of Mandy Llewellyn's (1980) inspirational piece – her very inconclusiveness is precisely what I find so appealing, especially her honesty about her struggles to locate her material. See Skeggs (1994).

10 This consensus is certainly corroborated by my finding this difference as a strong theme of girls' concerns.

11 See also the review of Gilligan *et al.* (1990) by Sara Delamont (1993).

12 Jane Miller's (1991) review of Walkerdine (1990) and McRobbie (1991) provides a useful context.

13 Whilst my knowledge of Australian English is limited and I do not know if the term 'slack' carries the expression of sexual looseness, I find it an interesting choice of words. If it does have those meanings it confirms my counter-interpretation that girls' moral ordering works *through* their appropriation of sexist (racist, classist) discourse and *cannot be abstracted from it* (see Chapters 4, 5, 6, 7). Indeed it is hard to see how girls' moral order would be able to remain uncontaminated in view of the ways in which masculinity, school, parental, community and state policing of girls precisely constructs girls sexuality as its object.

14 The recent flowering of popular and art house films with women's and girls' friendships as their theme suggests a need to qualify this general assertion, though we should note that most of these films have tragic and/or apocalyptic endings. In this context we can think of *Mina Tannenbaum* (1994 France/ Holland/Belgium); *Heavenly Creatures* (1994 New Zealand); and *Thelma and Louise* (1991 USA).

Chapter 2

RE/THEORIZING CULTURE:
GIRL SUBJECTS AND
GIRLS' SUBJECTIVITIES

Introduction

Carolyn Steedman's *Landscape for a Good Woman* is a book about, as she puts it, 'lives lived out on the borderlands, lives for which the central interpretive devices of the culture don't quite work' (1986:5). Engendering culture and theorizing girls' investments in its private forms involve a refocus. I propose to ground my understanding of girls as cultural agents of the 'borderlands' of feminine friendship forms. This version recognizes friendship as a social base for the elaboration of forms of social subjectivity (Morgan 1990; O'Connor 1992).

In taking up Johnson's definition of cultural studies as being concerned with 'the historical forms of consciousness or subjectivity, or the subjective forms by which we live or the subjective side of social relations. It includes centrally the "who I am" or "who we are" of culture, the formation of individual and collective identities' (Johnson 1986: 280–1), this account breaks with a reliance upon culture as sights and public forms to capture those more private and elusive moments when subjectifications are made the currency of feminine cultures of friendship.

Llewellyn (1980), despite her determined attention to the significance of girls' location in their cultures of friendship, actually misses the point about the particular effectivity of girls as conduits of power. It is *because* for girls social meanings are apprehended in so personalized a form that they are lived so intensively and contradictorily. You recollect the way Cordelia's task was constructed as one of 'improvement'.

The analytic trick is to refuse both the place of negation – of a model of culture in which girls/women are always somewhere else: 'Women were just the people over in the corner by the speakers' – and a position in which women are an essence. This demands an altogether more plastic and microscopic model of girls in groups. We need another language for reading girls' groups before we can situate a *social* as well as a material cultural understanding of girls in groups as friends; first, a recognition of the role of the private domain in education; second, the elaboration of the gendered dimensions of cultural hegemony and the role of girls' friendship in its installation; third, a recognition of the significance of subjectivity for reading girls' relations to each other and to their schooling; and lastly, it implies paying attention to the social and affective dimensions of girls' experiences as a way to capture both the shared as well as the differentiated aspects of girls in public school culture.

My argument insists upon seeing girls' (friendship) lives as invested in the production of certain forms of power and subjectivity. These regimes of connection/(micro) technologies of power then become analysable in historical and social terms as examples of what Eagleton (in another context) describes as sites for 'instilling . . . specific kinds of value, discipline, behaviour and response in human subjects' (1985/6:97). My reading echoes how Janet Holland conceives of the search to open up analytic space as a 'post-post modernism' which would:

Work across the tension between the concern with how experience and difference is known and made meaningful, and how and why experience is grounded in everyday life, material embodiment and real differences of power. It would form a link between the post modern conceptualisation of the construction of multiple subjectivities and gender and sexual identities in discourse and the experience of materiality, of being physical in the physical world.

(Holland 1995)

Susan Contratto (1994:374) also argues the relevance of an account which situates girls' bodies: 'The defining experience of adolescence is physical: puberty as an event and as a process is felt in the body in all sorts of complex ways'. My particular reading of 'embodiment' goes further because it also incorporates a recognition of the place of emotions (as material productions) in coercing or seducing as we 'make ourselves' into particular subject positions.

In studying girls at school it would be hard to miss just how much girls' feelings matter, not merely because they may signal distress but also because of their less obvious complicities with the production of their subjectivities (Emmerson 1993). The following sections develop these arguments in more detail.

Investing the borderlands; generating an analytic vocabulary for girls' cultures

Repositioning understandings of culture away from the coherencies of the visible – external and the public – entails showing how the public meanings of forms of power are produced in the everyday. It means a scaling down of our gaze to that level of culture which is enacted between individuals and groups in social contexts. However, the turn away from the grandiose is not a simple-minded endorsement of empiricism as a guarantor of truth; the aim is more that of trying to capture the situated meanings of the 'obvious'. In short, it is by paying attention to the discordant and unstable discourses of girls' talk, writing and associated material practices which provide information about how girls work through the personal. These knowledges are hinted at, but not explored, in Brown and Gilligan's (1992) concept of the 'underground', as well as representing one important modality of school based cultural hegemony (Ashendon et al. 1987).

The first place to create the analytic space which concerns us here, is Jane Miller's (1990) brilliant engagement with theories of culture and cultural re/readings. She indicates why there might be both some merit (as well as some problems) in returning to Gramsci to develop a more inclusive (gendered) account of culture. She begins by arguing that we urgently need to extend (or replace) a set of concepts which ground a masculine construction of 'civic society'. She asks, 'Why for instance, is Gramsci's use of the word "hegemony" at once so tantalisingly attractive to feminist analysis and yet so wholly under-developed in its potential relevance to women?'(Miller 1990:23). She notes that the lack of any conceptual elaboration of the notion of hegemony has severely limited our capacity to theorize those spaces and places rendered off limits in models of cultural and social hegemony – what Corrigan (1987:19) has called in a slightly different context, 'the buried, profane, fragmentary, diffused struggles around the signs of education (an ethnography of the Body of Schooling and its disciplinary contours, names and boundary maintenance policing) . . .'

Stephen Ball makes a related point in a recent defence of his theorization of the state; he argues that 'our theories of the "non-state", (what we might call) civil society, are superficial and simplistic' (Ball 1994:178). One could provocatively suggest that one reason for such simplicities is the lack of serious attention (by male left-wing academics) to the feminist insistence on seeing the private domain as redolent of cultural and political significance (see O' Brien 1987).

The neglect of those necessarily less public and more elusive themes of non-state civil society have their roots in the masculinist domination of theoretical and practical accounts of culture – a queasy alliance of the gang of lads inside the academy with the gangs of lads outside (Griffin 1995; McRobbie 1980). This is a tendency which is still prevalent. It has, for example, seriously restricted what can be said about the impact of education reforms (Arnot 1992; David 1993; Hey 1995c).

Miller's rereading of Raymond Williams exemplifies what is at stake in breaking with the current radical definition of culture. She stresses the strength of Williams's insistence on recognizing the 'sheer power and pressure of dominant culture':

> We could say that the essential dominance of a particular class in society is maintained not only, although if necessary, by power, and not only, although always, by property. It is maintained also and in-evitably by a lived culture: that saturation of habit, of experience, of outlook, from a very early age and continually renewed at so many stages of life, under definite pressures and within definite limits, so that what people come to think and feel is in large measure a re-production of the deeply based social order which they may even in some respects think they oppose and indeed actually oppose.
>
> (Williams 1989:74)

She shows, however, that Williams (in common with the male Left) confined his empirical, theoretical and fictional explorations of the lived world to the male world. Her resistance to the male (and one might add culturally hegemonic conceptualization of social class as masculine) enables her to trace the contours of a more woman (and girl) sensit-ive formulation – a gendered conceptualization of culture within which we could locate other important resources for the making of (class) consciousness.

The 'disruptive' presence of feminist texts – including Carolyn Steed-man's narrative of her mother's desires: 'My mother's *longing* shaped my own childhood. From a Lancashire mill town and a working class twenties childhood she came away wanting: fine clothes, glamour, money; to be what she wasn't' (1986:6, emphasis added) – indicate the issue here. Stories of working-class women's lives problematize the taken for granted privilege attached to paid work as *the* site for the foundation of working-class consciousness. Cathy Urwin's (1985) account of 'mothering', as well as Ruqaiya Hasan's (1986) work on cultural transmission, offer 'highly persuasive examples [of] exactly how women come to assume respons-ibility for transmitting the culture's most controlling articulations of gender division and difference' (Miller 1990:64–5).

Miller returns us to Gramsci's theory of hegemony and the tantalizing theme of her book – seductions – in reminding us of the private compli-cities and personal consents elicited through our participation in private cultures of intimacy 'learned at a very early age' within which we learn the lessons of distinction. Steedman acknowledges that 'it was women who told you about the public world, of work, of politics, the details of social distinction' (1986:33; see also Kuhn 1995). Miller (1990:22–3) hints at what a feminist reworking of the notion of hegemony might entail:

Gramsci's hegemony describes institutions and strategies of control in a class society, through which those in power elicit and receive the consent of those they govern. These strategies acquire some of the tension and the elasticity I have emphasised in my circling of seduction . . . So far I have concentrated on the overlapping meanings of seduction and hegemony. These words issue however from significantly different histories of use. Behind seduction lie the private, the hidden and personal, the secret, the sensual, the erotic, and pleasure. Gramsci's version of hegemony bestrides a map of metaphors involving force, and military conquest, massed and public and – inevitably – male belligerence. Yet the subtlety of Gramsci's appropriation lies precisely in his use of the word within an analysis of civil and potentially non-violent control.

Miller's pursuit of the metaphor of seduction implies that we can begin to supplement or trace an alternative gendered model of cultural hegemony within that realm in which seduction beckons – 'the private, the hidden and personal, the secret, the sensual, the erotic, and pleasure'. The theme of ideological seduction carries us into the terrain of intimacy, subjectivity, femininity and desire (which have been explored in discussions about motherhood and heterosexuality; Chodorow 1978; Leonard 1980; Gallop 1988; Ruddick 1990; Jackson 1995) but not, however through the realm of girls' relationships.

We have glimpsed, however, how the seductions of cultural hegemony are shaped by girls' co-investments in intimacy and difference; of how desires are worked through the pleasures of belonging; of how fears were instituted through not belonging as well as girls' different abilities to police or be policed by 'normality'.

The domain of desire, of the emotions, is noticeably the domain which feminist cultural theorists have (with staggering lack of success) insisted be brought within an account of the cultural. As Franklin and her co-authors (1991:176) noted, 'Looking at questions of reproduction as well as production, *Women take Issue* highlighted the need for cultural studies to engage with the "personal" dimensions of culture in the political context of a feminist analysis'. In pointing to the unevenness of the development of engagement between feminism and cultural studies and the continuing failure by male cultural theorists to fully comprehend the gendered nature of culture, these critics remind us of what is continually at stake for girls and women in making claims to be both seen and understood in cultures and their theorizations – that is, nothing less than ourselves.

'Outside any law of recognition': cultural il/legitimacy[1]

In her introduction to a collection of her essays, Carolyn Steedman makes the following observation:

My other argument with William's work is to be found in the essays entitled 'Prisonhouses' (Part I), 'Amarjit's Song' (Part II), and 'The Mother Made Conscious', (Part IV). There is a history of subjectivity (of the kinds of subjectivity that people have felt obliged to make for themselves in different historical circumstances) that can connect subjectivity to the ideas of culture. Both of these ideas have been organised around women . . . 'The primary effect of this alternative sense of the term "culture"', says Williams, 'was to associate it with religion, art, *the family and personal life* . . .' Indeed, in those five words lies occluded a whole history.

(Steedman 1992:13, emphasis in original)

Steedman (1982, 1985, 1986, 1992) situates her historical rereadings on the grounds of that occlusion bringing into view specific feminine contributions to cultural history – women as teachers; mothers and social reformers; female children as interpreters of their classed social worlds (see Kuhn 1995). As I have argued within Chapter 1 there is a persistent need to keep telling occluded stories. Steedman herself hints at the terrain,

We laughed a lot, cried a lot, wept over all the sad stories. An ongoing show of human variety . . . classrooms are places of gossip, places for the observation of infinite change, new shoes, new haircuts, a pair of gold earrings for pierced ears: passion, tears, love, despair.

(1985:8–9)

As a teacher I too often witnessed these 'infinite changes', frequently mopped away tears and lost count of the times the minutiae of girls' passions fractured the rhythms and flows of our official classroom routine. In a sense, nothing is surprising about these findings. What is more surprising is the lack of an analytical vocabulary to understand them. Steedman does not draw attention to the specifically gendered nature of the episodes she describes, though they are all instances of girls' cultural preoccupations at once so central to girls' definitions of themselves and each other – but also generally and widely excised in the schoolroom (Steedman 1985).

Recent feminist work on girls and schooling suggests how girls are 'subjected' to the social, through discourse and social practices (Walkerdine 1985; Davies 1989; Walkerdine and Lucey 1989; Jones 1993; Thorne 1993; Mac an Ghaill 1994; Rossiter 1994; Gordon 1995; Kenway and Blackmore 1995). There is also an associated attempt to situate a definition of femininity through the concept of positionality. Linda Alcoff's (1988) 'positional woman' is a million miles away from the Harvard Project's 'authentic' or 'silenced' girl; radical feminists' 'faceless bunch'; subcultural ethnographies' 'fag-heaps'; symbolic interactionism's girls with 'attitudes'; and moral philosophers' 'resisters'. Alcoff's model of positionality conveys a more complex concept of identity and selfhood through refusing an essentialized account of femininity:[2]

> the essentialist definition of women makes her identity independent of her external situation . . . The positional definition on the other hand makes her identity relative to a constantly shifting context to a situation that includes a network of elements involving others, the objective economic conditions, cultural and political institutions and ideologies and so on. If it is possible to identify women by their position within this network of relations, then it becomes possible to ground a feminist argument, not on a claim that their innate capacities are being stunted, but that their position within the network lacks power and mobility and requires radical change. The position of women is relative and not innate, and yet neither is it 'undecidable'. Through social critique we can identify women via their position relative to an existing cultural and social network.
>
> (Alcoff 1988:433–4)

My use of the concept of 'positionality' follows the work of Jane Kenway and Jill Blackmore in that it recognizes difference itself as one of the defining conditions of women/girls' positionality (Kenway and Blackmore 1995). Hence positionality is not only a concept of place and power, it is also a conceptualization of a discursive economy in which different groups of subjects can and do try to position and out-position each other through using their access to differential resources of social, economic and cultural power. Debbie Epstein's (1993:13) discussion of the potentiality of poststructuralist theory is apt: 'I would wish particularly to note that power is not always wielded through coercion, but often through discursive practices which people, as active agents within these practices either consent to or resist'.

Significant others: the case for feminine friendship as a site for the construction of subjectivities and subjectifications

> So the only things that are important are: my mum and dads (step and real dad) and Boys that's all I think of – oh yeah and clothes and what I look like and my family and Gabbie and my other close friends.
>
> (Amelia, working-class white girl, Eastford School)

The picture Amelia offers is conventional.[3] She represents herself in a nexus of different relationships: first as a daughter; second as a potential heterosexual girlfriend and, almost as an afterthought, as a (best) friend. Whilst the public identity as a daughter appears straightforward, the corresponding (and more private) role in girlfriendship requires cultural decontamination. She writes in a later entry:

> Gabbie phoned nearly every day. I'm really glad we got . . . I've got a best mate like her. I don't know what I would do without her, when she phoned and says she misses me and it's boring without me I get a warm glow over me. I'm really glad, she's my best mate (I'm not a lezzy or anything but it's just Gabbie is my best mate and if anything happened to her I'd cry myself to death. We argue some-times and she makes me mad sometimes but she's stuck with me if she likes it or not I'm stuck with her).

Amelia, in delicately negotiating the mismatch between private feel-ings and the public cultural code of heterosexuality (Rich 1980; Wilton 1993), resists as well as capitulates to the assumptions of 'compulsory heterosexuality' (Rich 1980). Despite her intimate insistence on the power of her feelings for Gabbie (which ironically mimic the tenor of a long-standing marriage – 'We argue sometimes and she makes me mad some-times but she's stuck with me if she likes it or not I'm stuck with her'), she also accommodates to the supervening 'hetero-reality' (Raymond 1986). Importantly though, it is this desired/feared position as girlfriend which introduces another element of self-surveillance – worries about 'what I look like' (Rowbotham 1973; Coward 1984; Rossiter 1994) con-stituting the terms of her subordination.

In an article entitled 'In/forming schooling' Philip Corrigan writes, 'The struggle for social identity is the struggle over what is to count, what forms are *proper*; what kinds of expression are *public and accepted*' (Corrigan 1987:19, emphasis added). How and on what basis is Amelia making her decisions about 'what is to count' and 'what kinds of expression are public and accepted'? Amelia feels compelled to survey her private self and 'get it right' for me. She is keen to ensure that I do not think her feelings 'abnormal'. Crucially, staking a claim to a private form of girlhood sub-jectivity (as best friend), made her an accomplice in misogynistic culture.

This is a book which tells the stories of how girls like Gabbie and Amelia construct cultures of feminine friendship in conditions of complex and overlapping forms of oppression. My narrative explores how girls' cultural resources of friendship are variously devised, deployed, experi-enced and evaluated. Its territory covers the dense relationship between forms of subjectivity produced in the privacy of girls' interpersonal lives and public forms of social power and regulation.

Like many of the girls I interviewed, Amelia had an intense internal life; she takes the business of her feelings very seriously. She had a section in her diary called 'Feelings' subtitled 'This is the page for when at school I feel horrible'. She had a secret code to record 'no bad feelings'. Amelia represents herself through relationships and the emotions they elicit: feelings of connectedness and desires; anxiety and separation; pleasures and pains. In thinking through the social processes of how girls take up their position in the private and the public as cultural actors, the following account necessarily problematizes how the divisions between the private and public have been constituted (Johnson 1986) and theorized (Miller 1990; Franklin *et al.* 1991).

Richard Johnson observes that relations of power structure the actual division into public and private realms of culture, noting the crucial significance of vernacular and private (working-class, female and other cognate marginalized) cultures as sites of alternative knowledges with the *potential* to challenge the current social divisions (see Ribbens and Edwards 1995). Johnson (1986:287–8) comments about the exclusion of subordinated cultural forms: 'It is not that they are naturally or necessarily private: it is a work of power to privatize them; the condescensions of the powerful, the secrecies of the oppressed'.

One particular effect of the 'privatization' has been the exclusion of consideration of the domain of the emotions and personal relations in the schooling literature (Richards 1990; Kenway and Blackmore 1995). One major aim of this book is to reinvest a sociology of schooling with a discussion of how the relational and the affective dimensions of schooling work as a crucial site in the circulation of notions of difference.

To do this requires evidence that the so-called private marginal realm of schoolgirls' friendships is a significant place where the 'social' is indexed. As I have suggested, the interpersonal recesses of schooling provide a material base where girls are both compelled (and determined) to make sense of each other and the forms of identity proffered/preferred by: home, school, community, popular and élite culture and male authority. It is between and amongst girls as friends that identities are variously practised, appropriated, resisted and negotiated.

In opening up girls' relations with each other to sociological scrutiny, the book addresses the paradox of why and how the visibility of girls as each others' important and significant others, is simultaneously confirmed and then displaced in multiple knowledge domains: vernacular common sense, public culture and the practices of schooling as well as the radical and feminist literatures which aim to characterize their interrelations.

I trace two episodes from my own schoolgirlhood to indicate why I have a particular emotional and political investment in understanding the power of girlfriends to position one through difference. Each episode features girlfriends and their (latent and manifest) power to define decisive moments in the construction of my sense of self.

Defining moments: 'becoming a snob; making a gendered class identity'

Schooling is an experience of interminable definition. Having failed the 11-plus (an 11-plus failure) I went to a secondary modern school. At 13, as a 'late developer' I was asked to retake the selection test. I refused. I did not want to leave my friends and risk the new environment of a grammar or technical school, where I would have to mix with 'snobs' (Payne 1980). I completed my stay at the secondary modern school.

In the final year of secondary schooling, my class – top set of the fourth year, 4AC (Academic and Commercial – a highly ambiguous 'discursive position' if ever there was one) – were encouraged to transfer to the local newly opened technical college.[4] I can recall most of the friends who made the move with me. I especially recollect Susan C and Ann M. I have had many 'best friends' but the one I remember most was Susan. She had blonde hair, violet-blue eyes and was brilliant at sport and I adored her.

At college I discovered another passion – studying (defined as a hard worker). However these two desires were irreconcilable. One day when we were walking to the bus stop, Susan told me quite bluntly that I had 'become a snob'. In a simple phrase she both exposed, as well as condemned, the fragile aspirational self that I had been putting together. My social construction as a class enemy was systematic. Former friends applied a series of powerful sanctions; a whispering campaign in class (references to what I looked like); abusive notices pinned on the class notice board and a withdrawal of friendship. I was devastated. Under these pressures I moved further towards Charlotte (a middle-class newcomer). This was ironic since it was my relationship with her that had been cited as the decisive evidence that I was 'on the turn'! Transferring attention to Charlotte seemed to confirm my changing identity. When the exam results were posted, there were only a couple of others in the class who had passed enough O levels to go on to a further education college. Ann, Susan and my other friends contrived to 'fail'. I left them behind (literally) as I moved on to a college in a nearby city. My persistence eventually led, via an academic route, to university and into a career in teaching.

I still reflect upon this incident and its aftermath. Had I betrayed my friends or had they betrayed me? The politics and pains of my class aspiration were played out in those relationships, by gendered cultural means and with specific cultural effects. A reclass(ifi)ed identity – refused at 13 but embraced at 17 – was produced within/against the girls in my group. Ever since then I have been fascinated about the meanings girls constitute through their relationships. Certainly I am only too aware of the passions and pains girls can inflict upon each other. What captures my imagination and intellectual curiosity is the way that girls' relationships mediate schooling and culture.

Returning to school first as a teacher and then as a researcher is thus also a return to that underground school girlhood. Indeed it was a feminine underground (Brown and Gilligan 1992) which was the means as well as the 'topic' of the study (see Chapter 3).[5] The data from my study of friendship amongst white working and middle-class schoolgirls confirms aspects of my own schooling. The girls could have been my friends (see Chapter 6). They did all of the things I remember doing (as well as some I didn't). They gossiped, wrote notes to each other, wrote poems, sang songs, and speculated endlessly about the private lives of teachers, pop stars and sports heroes. They retreated to the toilet as the only safe space. They got irate, peevish, angry and jealous. They cared passionately about each other, offering advice and support about the vexed business of parental, teacher and boyfriend 'management'. They also bitched, bantered and argued as if their lives depended on it. They spread rumours and sought out rumourmongers in turn. It was a life lived intensely through the divisions as well as the intimacies of friendship, through the differences as well as the similarities of power.

It is a commonplace to note that girls' subjectivity is heavily invested in relationships. (Gilligan 1982; Gilligan *et al.* 1990; Brown and Gilligan 1992; Roland Martin 1995). Whilst many commentators note the central importance to children of their peer relationships (Opie and Opie 1959; Woods 1983; Davies 1984; Cullingford 1991) and feminist research has shown the particular importance girls attach to their friendships (McRobbie 1978; McRobbie and Garber 1980; Wulff 1988; Griffiths 1995). Yet we know that most of this work is constrained by a theoretical framework which privileges masculinity and that one effect of this is that the classic feminist ethnographies of schooling (McRobbie 1978; Llewellyn 1980; McRobbie and Garber 1980) are unable to focus upon the finer grains of the felt texture of these relations because commentators stand outside of, rather than within, the dimensions of their terrain.

We are thus aware of complex local gender economies of schoolgirls' friendships and we have evidence of aspects of its social symbolism (Vik Kleven 1993a, 1993b). We know of the existence of the visible forms of girls' transactions – of sweets, clothes, and 'fad' items – but much less is known about the *specific and more invisible processes* of girls' interrelationships, despite the fact that researchers have indicated the central place of talk in its reproduction (Johnson and Aries 1983a, 1983b; Kennedy 1986; Coates 1996).

It is not surprising therefore that there has been a failure to understand how the nature of girls as each others' girlfriends secures particular effects of power. The following exchange from a different clique of friends at the same school illustrates one episode in the making of what Ashendon and his colleagues (1987), have called 'a school based cultural hegemony' – three upper middle-class white girls are ostensibly debating the relative merits of different shops:

Suzy: I think it's quite élitist Warehouse, well it's not élitist . . .
Barbie: I just don't feel ashamed going into there . . .
Suzy: [giggles in slight shock at Barbara's snobbery?]
Barbie: [undaunted] Because I get ashamed going into places like Chelsea Girl and even . . .
VH: Why?
Lara: Well, it's tatty and horrible . . .
Barbie: And it's just the sort of people that go in there that I don't like being . . . don't like being classed as one of them . . .

Debbie Epstein (1993:18) captures precisely how subjective co-investments in the business of 'othering' create the terms of cultural hegemony:

The development of subjective identities is both complex and important, and identities themselves are multi-faceted and contradictory. They are formed through a combination of available discourses, personal experience and material existence . . . All the major binary opposites (white/black; heterosexual/homosexual; male/female; bourgeois/working class etc.) rely on the construction of subjective identities on 'othering' those on the other side of the divide. It is by drawing boundaries and placing others outside those boundaries that we establish our identities.

It is by paying detailed attention to how girls make their identities through their talk and writing as they make their relationships with each other which allows us ways into showing how girls' networks are saturated by, as well as structured through, divisions of power. Making one's self as a girl means that these divisions are frequently lived as intense moments of self-consciousness and self-contradiction, involving feelings of simultaneously 'being with' whilst 'against' an/other – as Amelia writes 'I get a warm glow over me . . . (I'm not a lezzy or anything . . .) or as Barbie more straightforwardly asserts, 'I don't like being classed as one of them'.
The accompanying case studies of different girls' groups use conceptual language drawn from feminist cultural studies, poststructuralist theorization of subjectivity and discourse and feminist interpretations of linguistic practices, in an effort to hold onto how girls 'do the cultural' through the material practices of girls' friendship. It is through positions and places constructed, resisted and negotiated within the interstitial spaces of girls' interpersonal worlds which provides the site for the mediations between private forms of subjectivity and public versions, between the 'male', adult world of formal schooling and the lived moments of personal meaning. How else is one to understand the note that opened this book, the

Atwood text, my own autobiographical episodes, the diary entry of Amelia, and the following note exchanged between two girls:

1   *Katie*: Hello Katy. How are you?
2   *Katy*: I'm Ok. Don't you just reckon he would be so sexy in an annoyed mood?[6]
3   *Katie*: Please Please Please Please with cherries and ice cream on top will you stay at Emma's tonight.
4   *Katy*: No No No with a great big fat flying turd on top.
5   *Katie*: Well bye I'm going to Rye tonight see you on Monday.
6   *Katy*: Ok, Katie. Bye. Why must I?
7   *Katie*: Because I don't want to stay without you because I get home sick and I always wet the bed.
8   *Katy*: Not to worry. I'll phone you up and sing to you lullabies 'til you fall asleep and I'll buy you a portable potty with your favourite Donald Duck on the front.
9   *Katie*: Katy please I can't live without you. I might have nasty nightmares if you're not there to hold my hand.
10   *Katy*: You'll survive without me for just one littley bittley nightie wightie.
11   *Katie*: I am staying at your house tonight because if I don't you will be a gooseberry . . .

This is another note written by two 'inseparable' girlfriends. I found it almost by accident at Eastford School when a teacher sympathetic to the girls and my research discovered it after one of her lessons.

It is impossible to contextualize fully this piece of writing. Unlike the other notes in the ethnography, I was not there during its making. I have not interviewed the girls concerned. I think it more generative to consider it in terms of a particular discursive moment in the construction of a specific form of intersubjectivity – an exemplary instance, if you like, of a discursive cultural strategy. Below I offer a reading as an example of my poststructuralist interpretative strategy.

It is interesting to note that the first writer, Katie, puts her best friend, Katy, into the position of the all powerful 'mother/other' towards whom she makes her 'child' demands (Walkerdine 1985). The language parodies exactly the wheedling resistance of small children set in play in the struggle to control the all powerful 'mother'. Within this discourse, the 'child' (Katie), attempts a series of complex moves to control 'her mother' (Katy) who is resisting these powerfully felt claims. Any woman familiar with the micro-negotiations involved in managing the insatiable demands and appetites of small children will recognize the emotional pull of this discourse and the equally compelling resistances adult women deploy in response.

The child/daughter manipulates her 'mother' through the minefield of maternal guilt. She claims autonomy through rejecting her (5: 'Well bye I'm going to Rye tonight'). She produces herself as 'sick' (7); she says that she will have 'nasty nightmares' (9), whilst the 'mother' urges her compliance through trade-offs (8, 10) which permit her own autonomy. I read this fragment of girls' writing as a specific production of an 'acceptable' form of intimacy through which these two white working-class girls recognize, as well as celebrate, their pleasurable as well as irksome intersubjective interdependencies. The adoption of these voices represents a cultural solution to the public sanctions against girls' homosocial emotional connectedness.[7] Framing an account through the concepts of discourse and subjectivity (Walkerdine 1981; Davies 1989) locates girls' relationships as *processual, dynamic* and *contradictory* (Davis 1994).

Girls in enacting their schoolgirl friendship at a level beyond immediate surveillance have been exceptionally busy (culturally speaking) and ignored. Wolpe notes how girls take up classroom spaces differently from boys, suggesting girls' success at disguising their own subversion. Wolpe argues:

> Girls' resistance may occur in the way in which they dress for school; truancy and school avoidance while occurring amongst both boys and girls, may differ in accordance with how each group spends its time. *In the classroom girls' resistance takes a different form to the boys, they may be quieter and less physically active than the boys but they nevertheless resist school lessons.*
>
> (Wolpe 1988:151, emphasis added)

Here is one brilliant piece of 'girls' talk' which matches the criteria Wolpe cites. It occurs between two best friends, Nina and Sally (from Crossfield School, see Chapter 5). Nina is pondering her current relationship with her boyfriend Jamie. She is writing to Sally for advice:

> Dear Sally,
> I do feel a lot for him you know I do sometimes. I wish I hadn't started seeing him because when he doesn't bother with me it hurts so much . . . Sally, Mr Parkinson [her teacher] keeps looking at me, the stupid git, he is so thick!
> Love you lots and more. Nina

Sally replied:

> Thanks, Nina I know that you like Jamie a lot and I know he hurts you, but the best are always cunts.

Nina responded tersely:

> Quite true darlin'.
>
> (girls' note, Crossfield School)

Primarily constructed in interpersonal, as opposed to public space, through countless and immeasurable numbers of discourses (Johnson and Aries 1983a, 1983b; Frazer 1988; Hey 1988; Frazer and Cameron 1989), girls perform not only acts of resistance but acts of interrogation which are as important as they are invisible, fluid, epiphenomenal or ephemeral. If talk and text are their common sense currency as well as their determining conditions, the need is for a form of attention which can capture the business of appearing to be 'doing nothing'.

To explore these themes further I draw upon an ethnographic study, conducted in the mid-late 1980s of white working-class and middle-class girls in two London comprehensive schools – Eastford and Crossfield (Hey 1988). The sociologically compelling processes of girls' friendship will be demonstrated through selected case studies of different girls' networks (three set in Eastford and one in Crossfield). In these case studies I move to explore two primary dimensions: their internal and external configurations (first in terms of their history, social processes and social construction and second as sites for the construction of numerous boundaries against boys and 'other' girls). It is only through understanding these interpersonal relations along both axes that we can imagine their supercharged role in the construction of forms of schoolgirl feminine subjectivity.

Privileging girls' friendships is not to claim them for ethical vanguardism. We are not talking here of an alternative or preferential lifestyle – a feminine culture carved out on the moral high ground (Gilligan 1982), superior to but parallel with the nasty male world of schooling (Mahony 1985). The aim is somewhat more complexly and ambiguously conceived. Whilst the theorization of feminine cultures recognizes that girls' same-sex relations are deliberately and almost hermetically sealed off from the interactant effects of boys and adults, it does not claim that they are permanently uncontaminated (Cockburn 1986). Whilst the analysis recognizes that girls gain important escape from the tedium of being always 'just a bunch of girls' or 'that faceless lot at the back' within the terms of their own company, it ultimately refuses the notion of a 'better' because 'feminine' culture by attending to the real material difficulties and differences which girls' relations articulate.

The following chapter discusses the process of data-gathering as a prelude to the case studies.

Notes

1 This expression comes from one of my own particular cultural heroines, Carolyn Steedman (1986:142). She is talking about her relationship to her own mother but she places the phrase in a context where she goes on to discuss cultural

erasure and I like the resonances as a metaphor of exclusion, invisibility, misunderstanding and rage.

2 James Donald (1985:350) in a review article summarizes the terrain that is of interest to me here:

> Ernesto Laclau has recently announced 'the impossibility of society'. 'Society' is an impossibility in the same sense as psychology's 'individual' – a fiction necessary for the effective operation of a particular human science, but a fiction which can never get the full measure of the fluctuating practices and relationships which it attempts to fix . . . So just as we call the precarious ordering of the psychic 'identity' or 'the individual', 'society' is what we call this precarious ordering of the social.

3 I had asked several girls if they would keep a week's diary for my research project.

4 Presumably the double option worked like an insurance policy – if the academic don't get you the commercial will. In more literal terms the first suggested the optimistic destination of O-level at 'the tech', whilst the second more realistic position signalled the working-class aspiration of a 'glamorous' 'respectable' and 'feminine' job (see Sherratt 1983; Gaskell 1992; Skeggs 1994).

5 I develop the idea of a feminine underground in sociological as opposed to psychological directions, however.

6 'He' either refers to a teacher or another boy in the class?

7 The term homosocial is imprecise but evocative. It comes from Rich 1980.

Chapter 3

LEARNING YOUR PLACE: RESEARCHING INTO GIRLS' FRIENDSHIPS

Introduction

The data for this book is derived from a small scale participant observation study conducted in two city schools in the mid-late 1980s (Hey 1988). My first research site was Eastford School, a large mixed comprehensive set in a middle-class suburb. The second was Crossfield Girls' School, a smaller comprehensive situated in a predominantly working-class part of the same borough. Both schools taught the 11–18 age group.

Apart from my inexperience in conducting research, field relations at Eastford were also complicated by other factors: the circumstances of the school, the nature of the project (privileging girls) as well as by the choice of fieldwork methods (participant observation). Early field notes anticipated such themes:

> Felt foolish 'cos I couldn't recollect the names of all the staff with whom I'd just been liaising. I kept calling Mrs Harris, Mrs Taylor, *felt just like a new girl*, overwhelmed by the bureaucratic nightmares that schools are (to newcomers). Not only do you have to remember the [layout of] buildings but also: staff names; statuses; subjects; timetables; timings; routines; protocols and facilities.
>
> (field notes, Eastford)

Throughout my fieldwork I never quite managed to avoid this sense of being 'lost', literally as well as metaphorically suspended in a liminal space 'down among the women' – a location somewhere between childhood and adulthood (see Walkerdine 1985; Mandell 1991). In conditions of oppression, there are some tantalizing parallels therefore between 'becoming a girl' and 'becoming a feminist ethnographer' since both identities are necessarily wrested from the same contradiction, namely that in staking a claim to power we are threatened by loss of claims to femininity. As other female ethnographers have noted, being taken seriously as a field researcher is a condition that can just as easily be withdrawn as it can be granted (Warren 1988).

Certainly the tensions of doing fieldwork (at Eastford) derived more from the gendered contradictions of working within a school unused to the discourse of equal opportunities, as they did from working across generational boundaries (Griffiths 1995). It soon became evident that any woman outsider choosing to study girls was seen as problematizing the way the school treated its girls. If the context was dominated by unquestioned assumptions about masculine hegemony, then the simple tactic of deriding the research focus as 'feminist' cleverly insulated most of the senior male staff from its implications. I was confronted (like the girls) by the difficulties of 'learning a place' inside the school. In effect the 'discourse of derision' meant that I too, went underground.

This chapter discusses aspects of my research experience in terms of its indivisibility from the material collected. The fact that I was studying girls in schools through the axis of their privatized friendships meant that the project was read in two conflicting ways – as simultaneously non-serious but also as a threat. Additionally the social spaces I wanted to investigate and the type of questions I wished to explore were viewed not only by male 'gatekeepers' with a great deal of suspicion but also and perhaps not surprisingly by some of the girls (See Hey 1988, Chapter 1; 1994 for a fuller account).

'Downwardly going' and 'upwardly mobile': two schools

Eastford was a school in crisis. One specific focus of this during the fieldwork was the disruption caused by union action in response to a national dispute. Staff morale was low, partly as a result of falling rolls and the resultant threatened redundancies and partly due to the headteacher's inability to manage divisions amongst the staff. The demise of the school's status as a boys' grammar school (prior to its amalgamation with the girls' grammar school under comprehensivization) was still the cause of nostalgic regret by the hard core of 'old masters' from the earlier regime. The backwash of the decision to amalgamate and become comprehensive *still* resonated in attitudes to the 'comprehensive' as opposed to the 'élite' children. In contrast, there was a strong pro-comprehensive 'left' position held by the union activists. The split was further elaborated around the call for union action. The senior management team and the 'old masters' declined whilst the majority of the staff complied.

These differences undermined the school's capacity to police the behaviour of its pupils, a situation which was intensified at a time of industrial sanctions. This in turn increased the difficulties of working in the school, because the pupils had understood only too well that it was possible to exploit the weakness of the system. Many of the most disaffected and demotivated pupils of both sexes simply voted with their feet.

The divisions and resulting tensions within the staff were reflected in the existence of three interconnecting but separate staffrooms. Senior male teachers – grammar school old masters – occupied the quieter, non-smoking end and created an ambience which aspired to that of an Oxbridge common room. The middle room was the domain of the union activists, whilst the remaining room was occupied by the non-aligned, a mix of staff room 'wags' (Cunnison 1989) and crossword fanatics. The latter group were younger staff but it also included some older female part-time staff from the remedial department. I positioned myself with the relatively neutral group.[1]

Eastford School nevertheless enjoyed more advantages than Crossfield. It was located in a large expanse of playing fields near a prosperous residential area. Its intake still included many children from this affluent middle-class area. The other side of the school was fringed by some residual forms of corporate housing – post-war council estates. These estates provided most of the working-class pupils for the school.

Crossfield School was considerably more downmarket. It was situated near the site of a large gasworks built alongside the West Cross Canal, which had once been the basis of the area's industrial past. However, in the city, distinctions of class were highly volatile; some areas and indeed some roads were upwardly mobile and some distinctly downwardly going. Gentrification continued alongside dereliction in Crossfield, but the former had not yet erased the locality's proletarian character.

Crossfield School opened on its current site in the 1930s. The staff claimed it was closely identified with its neighbourhood and the predominantly female staff professed expertise in dealing with 'typical secondary modern' girls. The school ethos evinced a team feeling. However, like Eastford, there was also an eccentric subculture: 'school mistresses' who treated the 'gals' like 'young ladies'. This position, favoured by a particular generation of single women teachers, possibly reflected a class nostalgia for their own 'nice' girls' schools (Evans 1991).

Crossfield's origins had a continuing effect, not only upon the school's reputation (almost as elusive a concept as a girl's!), but also in depressing the aspirations of the majority of its pupils. The identity of the school as a local white working-class secondary modern school was however changing because of the recruitment of Asian girls. This new intake was not only more affluent than the school's traditional pupils, but also more ambitious. Crossfield was also proving more attractive to Eastford's affluent white middle-class, disenchanted by the falling reputation of their neighbourhood school.

The fieldwork was undertaken prior to the intensification of the marketization of education (Hargreaves and Reynolds 1989; Ball 1990; Bowe *et al.* 1992), nevertheless, both schools were already under market pressure. The borough had a recognized overcapacity in secondary school places, for example Crossfield contracted from six entry classes (11-year-olds) to four over four years (though this trend had halted), and Eastford had decreased from nine entry classes to five over five years. In the climate of disappearing pupils, the local authority's commitment to a policy of community education was viewed with cynicism in both schools.

'Class issues': methods and methodological difficulties in researching into girls' friendships

> Very seldom does a start up sampling frame survive the lovely imperfection and intractability of the field. It must be bent and reframed.
>
> (Miles and Huberman 1984:38)

As the writers suggest, research in the real world is lived as a series of rapidly unfolding and occasionally unpredictable events about which one has to make practical decisions (Mandell 1991; Skeggs 1994). The fact that I had to recruit other girls to the study (from another school) reflected the power of male gatekeepers rather than the original intention (which was to make a one-site study).

In the process of implementing my research strategies I had also to make less dramatic compromises. These involved renegotiations about access to take account of the implacable routines of institutional life. Certainly my negotiations at Eastford were full of 'lovely imperfection' shaped as they were by my increasingly desperate attempt to find a suitable cohort of girls with whom I could spend a sustained period of time. There were two main dimensions to this. The first related to the formal mechanisms of schooling as an institution and the second concerned the girls' own informal responses to the school system and to me.

Any study of self-selecting groups like friends cuts right across the administrative divisions within formal settings like schooling (see Griffiths 1995). The devices of the curriculum (subject specialization, academic differentiation, setting/streaming and the complex patterning of subject option choices) constitute public as opposed to private groupings.[2] My original intention to study older pupils proved impractical.

The only solution was to move down the age range. I thus solved the problem by choosing Ms Spencer's class (1S). My inexperienced trial and error approach (dipping in and out of classes while trying to establish access) was inadvertently beneficial. It was through visiting different groups and different classes that I had become visible throughout the school.

Despite settling upon Ms Spencer's class, I was able to include (in the study) a variety of girls from the older age groups. In the course of my year at Eastford, I developed a close alliance with Carol, Gabbie and Amelia (white working-class 14-year-olds). I was additionally 'befriended' by numerous other working-class girls, though I researched these girls in a less systematic (and more opportunistic) way. These included various groupings of girls who talked with me in the playground, the cafeteria, and the nearby park or café (Liz, Michaela, Melly, Candy, Dottie and a whole host of other third, fourth and fifth year girls. Approximately 20 of these girls completed a diary for one week recording their social activities.

At Eastford, my most systematic classroom observations featured the girls in Ms Spencer's class of 11-year-olds, where I focused upon three networks of girl friends: 'the little élite group' of Erin and her best friend Samantha, Anna and her 'best friend' Saskia, and a looser grouping of Olga, Clara and Tamara who were part of, but not so central in, the clique.[3] All the girls were white and middle-class. Most of these girls were ostensibly prospering academically, though there was concern about Saskia's 'attitude' and Anna's 'ability'.

I also interviewed two close friends – Sonia and Iris – who were white working-class girls, so close that they coordinated absences. Additionally I got to know Natalie who was African-Caribbean and Laura from an Anglo-Portuguese background. Both girls were working-class. Kay (middle-class and white) arrived in the class halfway through the term but had a prior affiliation with a girl in another form and I did not get to know her well.

I undertook participant observation in Ms Spencer's class for approximately three terms, and followed the girls' transition into the second year, where they still had the same form tutor. I interviewed Ms Spencer, several senior members of staff and some of the year heads. I deliberately tried to keep my gaze upon the girls but could not avoid becoming familiar with some of the dynamics of the boys' relationships, as well as aspects of the gender dynamics between the boys and the girls.

At the same period I followed a parallel formation of girls also known as 'the little élite group': Lara, Barbie and Suzy.[4] These were fifth years – white upper middle-class, academically oriented 14- and 15-year-olds. These friends pursued a very similar academic curriculum, and like the other clique I tracked them as they moved into a higher year.

There were additional complications about tracking working-class girls higher up the school. Class at Eastford was literally strongly correlated with social visibility. In short, the older working-class girls were frequently absent. This affected my fieldwork decision-making in several ways.

Tracing an ethnography of girls' friendships both necessarily, as well as accidentally, tracks girls' multilevelled exploitation of school. My study records the degree to which girls variously experienced, as well as constructed, their own investments in its multiple possibilities. Was school seen as a social site for meeting friends as well as a source of academic prestige, status and display? Or alternatively was it predominantly the source of boredom, antagonism, disappointment and general social disempowerment, which only the solidarity of one's close friendships redeemed (Corrigan 1987)? Correspondingly, research access to these various responses will map how, where and in what sense girls are invested in school, invested in schooling and friendship, invested in becoming particular sorts of girls (and indeed invested in cooperating with social researchers).

The more 'academic' or middle-class the girls, the more observable they were in classroom situations. 'Regular' girls meant for regular school observations. The most sustained classroom observations were thus of 'the little élite groups' (see Chapter 4 especially) and the most fragmented was of Jude's 'typical girl's group' (see Chapter 5), except paradoxically for the week when she and her clique agreed to my 'shadowing' them. It was then pointed out to me that this was the only week when all the girls in her clique were present.

Opportunistic attendance called up a creative not to mention a pragmatic response. My relationship with Carol (a white working-class girl) at Eastford was characteristic of my countering tactic of opportunistic observation. I had to make myself available when she visited the school to sign on for morning or afternoon registration. Once we had rendezvoused she (and I) would disappear into the school surroundings. She only ever went to lessons when she liked the teacher (see Chapter 6 for a fuller discussion of our field research relationship).

Conversely classroom observations of Suzy and her friends (the fifth year 'little élite group' was apparently easier but contrarily, the least rich in terms of generating data about how their friendship worked inside formal schooling. Being invested in the official business of schooling meant for these particular girls drawing boundaries about their interpersonal relations, a response which the working-class disaffected girls were simply not interested in emulating.[5] Most of my data on the older middle-class girls came from informal interviews and their personal talk as well as our 'conversations' (see Chapter 7). In short, the social conditions of data-gathering on girls' friendships in schooling reflected the relations of class and gender through which it was constituted.

Public and private resistances: accessing the borderlands (1)

Negotiating appropriate points of entry and sustaining access implicated the power of the school to control the social experiences of its girls through its gatekeeping practices, as well as the specific power of girls to block forms of intrusion. Both prohibitions rehearsed different gendered aspects of researching into the marginalized cultures of girls in school. I look first at the formal (adult) official response before discussing some issues which emerged in the context of how girls themselves read my research interest.

There was (as I have indicated) a general cultural relegation of girls as a group in Eastford School, though this was mediated by class and race (achieving white middle-class girls were noted as being exceptional). This fact not withstanding, girls' general marginalization at Eastford was expressed in a variety of practices and ranged from their unexplored absences, through to their harassment in non-traditional subjects, as well as in their lack of safety in the surrounding community. Researching into girls' lives at school invariably presented other opportunities for the exercise of masculine powers, most noticeably shown in how the senior male teachers publicly positioned the research project and in their subsequent efforts to restrict access.

Contracting research relationships at Eastford at a time which coincided with teachers' industrial action was just the wrong sort of luck common in fieldwork. Good will, essential to social organizations and their study, had almost evaporated. My negotiating position was not helped because my research question was understood as 'feminist research' and therefore construed as potentially subversive. One way the staff managed my actual presence was through parody. Shortly after my arrival the following 'advert' was circulated in the school bulletin: 'Item 411: "I have not found so great faith no, not in the whole of Israel". In pursuit of her research into Further Aspects of Femininity, Valerie Hey will be observing 3C . . . [etc.]'. On another occasion a physics master said about the same girls: 'You'd get more response from a brick wall. The best of luck!'

Allied to this were deeply embedded presumptions on the part of the boys (who outnumbered the girls by approximately two to one) that they were the most important people within schools (Mahony 1985; Clarricoates 1987; Griffiths 1995). When one of the boys in a class challenged my right to study girls he was apparently told by the form tutor that 'social researchers study very bizarre subjects'. The teacher cited, as an example, someone she knew who was looking at 'fish symbolism in Shakespeare'. It is however also plausible that male resistance to being ignored expressed both boys' jealousy as well as power.[6]

During the course of the fieldwork I experienced some harassment – 'stare-outs' and mild verbal abuse from a few boys, who it seemed to me had taken upon themselves the role of conveying collective male disapproval. However this was manageable. What was less easy to manage was the dilution of access by their male elders.

Half-way through the fieldwork at Eastford, the headteacher summoned me to his room. He argued that my presence was proving too disruptive. He claimed that several male teachers found my presence in classrooms (I was sitting at the back with the girls) uncomfortable. He then conceded that if I wanted to continue talking with the girls I had to do so in their time but not in the school's. The head pointed to the disruption already caused through the teacher sanctions. He then secured this new access negotiation through offering me the opportunity to go into Crossfield School, where the head was a friend of his.[7]

I remember being comforted in the midst of these alterations by the first maxim of Halcolm's Evaluation Laws: 'Always be suspicious of data collection that goes according to plan' (reported in Patton 1990). In reality I managed to hold onto my research relationships (both inside and outside classrooms) at Eastford. This was achieved ironically through the practical assistance provided by numerous feminine friendship networks. Female members of staff and groups of girls persisted in talking with me, the staff letting me into their lessons and the girls continuing to tell me about themselves. Feminine marginalized cultures of social support became the means as well as the content of the research. However, establishing this base had not been without its own problems.

Ethnographic practices and cultural lessons: accessing the borderlands (2)

As I stated earlier, research is invariably accomplished by an uneven struggle against the messy complexities of life. Apart from having to overcome (or work around) official suspicion I also was confronted by unofficial opposition. No wonder Martyn Hammersley once remarked that 'Research was like a voyage of discovery where you spend most of your time out at sea'.

In electing to study girls and their cultures I was already committed to accessing precisely those spaces designed to keep intruders out. Other researchers have noted the material impenetrability of girls' social networks:

Boys flock; girls seldom get together in groups above four whereas for boys a group of four is almost useless. Boys are dependent on masculine solidarity within a relatively large group. In boys' groups the emphasis is on masculine unity; in girls' cliques the purpose is to shut out other girls.

(Henry 1966:150)

Certainly there were few scripts available for conducting an empirical sociological investigation into girls and their friendship. Mandy Llewellyn (1980:44) captured the challenge precisely when she wrote:

Once I had entered the field I encountered a mass of problems and dilemmas, some of them generally related to this style of research, others more specifically concerned the focus of my study. These latter involved the difficulties of gaining some sort of purchase on the privatized, fairly excluding spheres inhabited by adolescent girls.

This section traces the complications associated with researching across the public and the private domain. It specifically focuses upon how girls' relationships are, as McRobbie and Garber pointed out, 'well insulated' so that they can 'effectively exclude not only other "undesirable" girls but also boys, adults, teachers and researchers' (1980:222).

One incident condensed for me what is at stake for girls in making themselves available for adult scrutiny in such conditions.

Desperately seeking Sandra?

It is assumed I think, that even if women researchers know girls are 'excluding', sharing a gender provides grounds for rapport (Oakley 1981). Indeed, feminist researchers warn against the exploitative potential of female/female field relations (Finch 1984; Stacey 1988). My own initial encounter demonstrated the opposite – the fragility of rapport between researcher and researched. As a new girl in the field and as a new girl at school I made mistakes. I cite one instance which taught me a great deal about how girls exercise power through the veto of exclusion as well as the structured antagonism arising from class relations.

At Eastford School I was originally sponsored by the head of the English department. She suggested to me that I might like to initiate my study through shadowing Sandra, a white working-class girl in her fourth year. I was told that Sandra was 'interesting'. I approached Sandra and explained my study and asked if I might 'go around' with her and her friends the next day to get to know her. She seemed keen, and appeared to have consented and I smugly congratulated myself on the success of our affinity. I arranged to meet her the following day, and went to collect her from her classroom. I was met by Sandra behaving as if I was a known social outlaw. 'It's that woman!' she yelled, running to the back of the classroom, seeking protection from her teacher. I retreated mortified by embarrassment, and muttered something incoherent to the bemused teacher and her class and disappeared into the sanctuary of the girls' toilets – one of the few private places in the school (see the girl in Cullingford 1991:52).

I had not attended to the gaps between what is said and what is meant. I had not been sufficiently self-reflexive, forgetting both my adultness (Prout and James 1990; Solberg 1992; Morrow 1993; Thorne 1993), and my class status (Hey 1988). Sandra educated me. Clues about how

Sandra might have framed my intentions were abundant, but I had missed them. Earlier, in our first conversation I asked her how she spent her spare time. She told me that she went 'wally watching' (that is, looking at the local middle-class culture vultures) at the local arts centre. Anyone who has this view about the voyeuristic pleasures of social observation of the other has clearly worked out the costs of being positioned as the object of the (sociological) gaze.

This particular incident not only sensitized me to the particular salience of class antagonism at Eastford but it promoted my recognition of the imperatives of divisions and difference as the prevailing terms through which girl subjects also learned their place. It was here in the field, in 'among the women' that schooling's denial and mystification of power and difference emerged to forcefully invest girls' cultures. Marginalizing the discourses of power merely intensified the social and psychological investments girls had in securing, through their friendship, places for themselves which *did* at some level acknowledge the lived significance which the school so ferociously displaced and denied (see Chapter 8).

Engagingly therefore, girls' discourse of difference operated most powerfully in precisely those spaces into which I had been confined: the backstage of classrooms; the periphery of schools; the playing fields; the local off-site amenities; the cemetery; the local cafe; the shops; the canteen, and the school yard. It was outside of, or 'underneath' surveillance that the girls could best pursue their social task of discovering who they were inside their same-sex relationships.

Becoming marginalized placed me in precisely those same locales as the girls I was studying. Furthermore, as I have intimated, the margins of both schools were highly generative spaces dense with important sources of counter-information and counter-identifications. It was in many ways precisely the place to be. Recognition was one thing, access, as the Sandra incident reveals, another. Negotiating with the girls demanded methodological creativity, and most of all the capacity to secure and sustain their trust (Measor 1985).

Field relations: trading in femininity – talking to the girls

Surviving marginalization at the same time as researching it emphasized the reliance one has upon those who are being studied. This research therefore was only made possible through the sponsorship of key individuals, most notably that offered by Saskia, Carol and Suzy (at Eastford) and Jude (at Crossfield).[8] These alliances were further embedded by my participation in the public spaces of the school as well as private (girls' locker room) cultures.

In the course of the fieldwork I played rounders; went on cross-country runs; attended registration/pastoral time; stood around on fields at play-time; ate in the cafeteria; sat in on swathes of lessons; occasionally visited the staffroom; went to school plays and end of term demob cere-monies and leavers' assemblies. Rushing around covering the official as well as the more illicit of girls' activities demanded, at 35, a certain stamina as well as a willing suspension of disbelief on the part of both the girls and myself. It was required not only by the demands of parti-cipant observation but also as a test of my commitment to the girls. I did draw the line occasionally (and so did the girls) but mostly I boldly went where the girls in my study boldly went, even if this meant bunking or going behind the bike sheds (so they could have a smoke). Inter-estingly and significantly the trial of my acceptability as a researcher (that is, that I would not tell the teachers) replicated the social tests of girls' friendships (see Llewellyn 1980; Horowitz 1983; Hey 1988; Griffiths 1995).

My fieldwork effectively involved a series of complex trade-offs (Skeggs 1994). In the course of the study, the girls and I developed an implicit microeconomy of exchange and barter. The girls provided access to their social lives in return for certain tangible goods: my attention; advice; sweet money; access to a warm room; or absence from lessons (see Skeggs 1994). These small trades are endemic in most field relations but because they smack of the marketplace there is very little reference to them and like a lot of the 'housework' of research, these details seldom surface in research reports or theses (though see Oakley 1981).

In the course of my time in the schools I got to know about 50 girls reasonably well, 20 of these girls very well and three sufficiently well to have been invited to their homes and to have invited them to mine. One girl even sent me a note during a lesson. Others kept up communication after I left the schools, updating me on their present situations (see the correspondence in Chapter 6). Yet other girls sent me notes which they had stored away; others offered me diaries to read, I offered mine in return.

I only managed my study through the immense tolerance of the girls who accommodated me during lunch hours, free time at breaks, morn-ing tutor times and who invited me home when they had been sent off the premises as a result of the no-cover action. There were girls (like Carol) who took me in hand and showed me the ropes, who let me tag along with them on their jaunts to the local prom and recreation ground. Neither I, nor my stomach, will ever forget our many visits to the Pond Cafe safe refuge for so many of Eastford's working-class school refuseniks. However, willingness to indulge researchers is frequently constituted from the conditions of subjects' relative powerlessness (McRobbie 1982b).

A similar concern surfaces in this study. The girls' general tolera-tion of a nosy intruder (Sandra notwithstanding) signified a potentially exploitative situation. Such conditions are an implacable fact of research-ing on those less powerful than oneself (see Measor 1985).[9] Looking back at my practice and accounting for my decisions, the issue as I see it of breaking the pretence that one can somehow (singlehandedly) dis-solve the contradictions (of being a feminist working on girls' relative powerlessness) has meant my acceptance that research relations are nec-essarily made in, and constituted by these conditions of difference.

Despite seeking to establish non-exploitative field relations, I was never able to evade the facts that as a white woman with a middle-class educa-tion not only was I generally more powerful than most of the girls but my agenda was in part to appropriate parts of their lives for my own use (see Measor 1985). This is not to represent girls as powerless – in this I endorse Beverley Skeggs (1994) who also argues that girls' actions are about contesting power within terms which recognizes the force of social divisions.

Taking up this position is much more uncomfortable than assuming the orthodox cosier fantasy of imagining that our feminism secures for us the privilege of 'becoming one of the girls' through wishing away the differences between us and them. What is required is not only more reflexivity (about who 'we' are) but also a more finessed sense of how these power relations (including those of research) shift and are con-tested by their subjects/objects in the everyday (Davies 1989; Hey 1994; Patai 1994).

In terms of my own practice I tried to be as clear about what I was up to as I felt was appropriate. But at all times during the research the girls knew that I was a researcher and that I was observing their inter-actions (even though rumours circulated that I was variously a social worker, headteacher, probation officer, police officer or someone's mum).

The debate about ethics is one of the most engaged and detailed within feminist methodology; there is a vast literature (Oakley 1981; Stacey 1988; Opie 1992; Holland and Ramazanoglu 1994; Skeggs 1994). Inevitably issues of ethics become intensely focused when one is researching across the boundaries between the public and the private. As Johnson elo-quently puts it, 'To render such accounts public is immediately to activ-ate all the relations of power we traced . . . especially where the practice crosses the major cultural differences' (Johnson 1986:302).

I too, am acutely aware of this dilemma, since insisting on moving the cultural backstage (of girls and schooling) to the front stage (particularly at this time when the mainstream research gaze is mesmerized by the government's agenda), opens up not only a proverbial can of worms for the dominant but also, as I have hinted, for feminism(s). My stance certainly (re)activated as well as captured/disrupted the dominant forms of power and their circulation since what was discovered was not, as other researchers imagine, 'collective images of a non-subordinated sense of self' (Ribbens and Edwards 1995:255) but precisely the conditions of contradiction and oppression (as well as their refusal) within which girls and ourselves live.

The point of my move to uncover the workings of power in the culture was not to search for a return to a buried originary feminine realm beyond the world of oppression (Brown and Gilligan 1992; Ribbens and Edwards 1995; Roland Martin 1995) but to tease out the ways in which girls (and by analogy women) consent to, as well as resist, the multiple forms of subordinations, as well as to identify and analyse those occurrences when girls subordinate and oppress each other. Girl–girl social relations (as I have hinted) constituted a gendered (and hence collective) cultural code (see Frazer and Cameron 1989). However this was not easily appropriable, since it was one of the conditions of girls' general cultural subordination that rendered girls' investment in privacy, secrecy and intimacy and each other. Therefore it was only through moving into the same covert realm where girls managed their relations that it became possible to understand how the borderlands worked as *private* feelings, *personal* affiliations and *personal* writings – where 'difference(s)' (if you like) could be traced in how girls (privately) lived their own antagonistic relations with and against each other. I take the view that furthering our understanding of girls means we have to occupy the interstitial spaces of schooling to reflect upon the cultural power activated there.[10] A defining moment in this research dilemma was when I discovered the significance of note-writing.

In/significances: a methodological and ethical note on schoolgirl notes

The significance of girls' notes only impressed itself on me after I had been involved in the research for several months. In so far as teachers noticed girls' extracurricular activities they called girls' notes 'bits of poison' or 'garbage'. Girls referred to them as 'bits of silliness'. As far as I was concerned they were sociologically fascinating because they were important means of transmitting the cultural values of friendship.

It emerged that not only did these writings constitute visible evidence of the extensive emotional labour invested by girls in their friendships, they also comprised a 'pocket ethnography' of girlfriend work.[11] The correspondences materialized particular aspects of girls' interpersonal relationships to confirm that girls produced the private, encoded by feminine forms of power (Walkerdine 1985).

A typical note would take the form of a piece of writing addressed to a specific girl. (Ninety per cent of what girls wrote about concerned their own relations with each other – only a few spoke about boyfriends). The note was then passed more or less surreptitiously to the recipient who would then write back. The original author would respond and so on. Other girls would act as postwomen, circulating the document between the correspondents.

In the course of my study I collected over 50 correspondence sequences from Erin and Saskia's group at Eastford School. From Crossfield School I collected about 20 others, predominantly from within Jude's group. I did not see boys engage in this activity. Evidence from other research indicates that boys do different things both in classrooms and within their friendships. (Stanworth 1981; Mahony 1985; Connell 1987:85).

The struggle to take these notes seriously owed something to the difficulties of purloining these 'secret writings'.[12] Girls were experts in these 'invisible' communication activities, and only a few teachers ever noticed them or wilfully intervened to eliminate them. Scrabbling around on the floor after double maths to retrieve the discarded letters was hard to explain to another adult. One of the teachers I spoke with scooped them up out her classroom dustbin to offer them to me, saying that they were 'little bits of garbage'. Becoming, as one colleague described it, 'an academic bag-lady' is at odds with the notion of research as a serious scientific endeavour.

Sometimes girls just left them on desks or floors. Towards the end of my year in the schools, I asked my key informants for any they might have retained, not expecting any response. To my surprise they provided me with more examples. Some of the girls had stored them for four years or more (see for example the 'transgressive' text between Sally and Jude, discussed in Chapter 5).

Equally, converting the 'garbage' into data presents other problems. The raw material persists in being the opposite of what data is supposed to be. Everything about this material conspired to render it unavailable as data. The word data carries sedimented meanings about self-importance and substantiality. And yet they retained for me sociological interest not least because some of these notes took the form of correspondence chains that lasted a week and included over 50 separate exchanges. The girls' notes were intentionally 'marginal'; for example, they were written on the margins of other more official writing. A number were written on the back of rough drafts of schoolwork. They were often difficult (if not impossible) to decipher. If I had not also been attending to the flux of the girls' friendships through observations and interviews I would have had little purchase upon their actual sequence, let alone their importance. That they are important, if fragmentary, moments in the making of schoolgirl selves is explored further (see Chapters 4 and 5 especially).

Race and ethnicity

Since I had decided that the main method of my study was to be participant observation I anticipated that as a white woman I would be far
less likely to find acceptance in black and Asian girls' groups (see Edwards
1990 for another discussion of this, though she made a different decision). This means that what I have to say about girls' same-sex relations
cannot be extended to account for how various groups of black or Asian
girls do their friendship work.

My pragmatic methodological choice had important theoretical rami-
fications in that it meant that I was able to access the workings of how
girls constructed forms of white working-class racism (see Hewitt 1986;
1993).[13] It soon emerged that the racial and racist divisions between girls
at Crossfield School (see Chapter 5) were policed through the social
pressures exerted within friendship groups (see Remmington 1983 for
another discussion of ethnic and racial divisions in the field).

Conclusion

This chapter has described aspects of the social ecology of Eastford and
Crossfield Schools. It has also rehearsed some of the methodological difficulties and dilemmas of doing research into girls' cultures. Whilst diverse
settings of different girls' groups provide contexts which shape girls' class,
ethnic and cultural differences, more intriguingly, as we will see in the
rest of the book, it is girls' shared investment in the taken for granted
practices of feminine friendship that successfully disguises girls' own
roles in the co-production of difference.

The following chapters trace case studies of particular friendship networks through focusing upon social sequences concerned with their making, disputation or dissolution. The first one concerns the struggles about
who could claim to be a friend in one small clique of middle-class girls
in Eastford School.

Notes

1 Reinharz (1992) has a good overview of the wide-ranging literature about
  the respective arguments about appropriate distance and other matters relating to the ethics of research. See especially Chapters 2 and 3.

2 There is of course a relationship between the two – as most studies of girls'
  friendship note – that is, there is a marked tendency for girls to make friends
  with girls who they perceive as being like themselves. This is obviously
  related to the opportunity to make friends with girls who you are positioned

with at school but it is also driven by the girls seeking out similarities (see later in this book).

3 'The little élite group' is a term adopted by their teacher. I retain it because it speaks to their place in the class cultural hegemony.

4 Their teacher also called these girls 'the little élite group'. Lara withdrew from the study halfway through but her friends continued to participate.

5 Jude's notion of 'talking about something really interesting' condenses her approval of the content of her friends social talk as opposed to 'settling down to work'. See Chapter 5.

6 See Reinharz's discussion of gendered field work relations (1992:58–64) See also (Warren 1988) on the complexities of gender in fieldwork settings. It is fascinating to note that just as some boys were publicly annoyed because I *wasn't* studying them, some girls were annoyed because I *was*!

7 At Crossfield School the politics of access were mercifully much more straightforward. I was made welcome, introduced to the whole school and having explained my project, introduced to Judith. Jude, as the gatekeeper of her working-class group, created the circumstances of a far easier enculturation into the school. Her group consisted of: Jude and Gina (best friends), Maureen, Nina, Sally and Frankie. These latter four represented a much looser configuration. All the group were frequent absentees (see earlier), but given the terms of my initial contact the girls were willing to accommodate me outside as well as inside school. I spent about six months with this group. All the girls were white.

8 The discussion of trust and sponsorship in Griffiths (1995) is a recent and thoughtful example of the personal and intellectual demands of doing an ethnography, as well as exploring the reliance we, as fieldworkers, have upon the tolerance and help of girls.

9 Actually it is even more complex than simply asserting my absolute power over all the girls at all the time: Sandra made up her own mind: Lara withdrew from the research; even the most marginalized girls told me to leave situations where my presence was not welcome. At another level it is not satisfactory to simply locate myself as a middle-class feminist either; I come from a background very similar to a lot of the white working-class girls I was studying; certainly I often found my sympathies tested just as much by the bourgeois girls despite (on other occasions) being aware that the discourse of equal rights feminism was something that was a lot easier to share with the middle-class groups. In short I am saying that power, rapport and social relations are lived as complexly in the field as in life!

10 For example, it became clear that girls' use of personal knowledge about each other constituted key cultural resources of power. This requires us to acknowledge just what it is some girls do to each other by appearing to be 'merely' making or breaking friends.

11 Weiner (1976:11) cites an example of pursuing apparently insignificant leads.

12 Looking up less attractive words to describe my actions in a thesaurus dissolves the ethically safer euphemism I have chosen to gloss this act. The hidden meanings are filch, pinch, plagiarize, embezzle, poach. This neatly dramatizes the voyeuristic nature of the ethnographic gaze and its frequent dissolution and denial in *post hoc* rationalizations.

There is evidence for the existence of a related though not identical 'secret writing' practice in China. Women in Jiangyong County apparently developed their own form of writing in the course of which they wrote about themes important to themselves to cement their 'sworn sister' status (Minolin 1986). See also Chapter 8.

13 Inevitably the representation of black and Asian girls in some senses replicates the problems I addressed in Chapter 1 concerning the ways in which girls were made to appear in male ethnographic texts. I in no way want to imply that Asian or black girls were simplistically 'victims' – indeed the Asian girls at Crossfield organized themselves to seek action about their experience of racial abuse. Neither am I unaware of the related problems of publicizing Jude's clique's racism. I discuss this in context in Chapter 5.

Chapter 4

MIDDLE-CLASS GIRLS MANAGING THEIR DIFFERENCES

Introduction

> the day I made friends with Alexia. This is only one of the
> many good days I remember, but this was one of the best
> because everyone wanted to be her friend, and I was sort of
> chosen. She was pretty and good natured, she never got angry
> and she was the only person I have known, other than maybe
> Samantha, who was like this.
>
> (Tamara [1S], extract from an essay entitled
> 'The Best Day of My Life')

Tamara's key terms are as conventional in their own way as Amelia's (see Chapter 2). 'Pretty', 'good-natured' and never getting angry also reflect subject positions for 'good girls' proposed by girls' popular fiction (Walkerdine 1984) as well as those preferred by schooling (Walkerdine 1985). This ideological convergence on 'niceness' as a repertoire of ideal girlhood was an assumption held by most of the girls' teachers, and which the girls in their turn were well aware and against which they had to contend.

The emotional demands of becoming a friend and making someone into your own special friend frequently demanded defiance of the injunctions about 'niceness', however (see Griffiths 1995 discussion of the 'nasty' girls' group). When this happened girls had to confront the fact that teachers (and others) were commonly given to pathologize their investments in this institution (Griffiths 1995). Girls' failure to keep their relations with each other under proper social regulation, that is invisible, often meant that when their relationships emerged into public scrutiny they usually did so as discipline problems. When I asked a year head about the impact of friendship on girls, she replied, 'There are a lot of instabilities, bitching and changing around. I have to move people from groups'.

Teachers' hostility towards girls 'emotionality' provided an especially awkward context when young middle-class élite girls were involved in disputes with each other. The pressure to construct the feminine bourgeois ideal as the capacity to never get angry presented particular difficulties. The following case study captures how one small élite clique contended with their feelings, as well as their desires, to hold onto that ideal place.

'Being nice' and 'being bossy' – the management of dis/order amongst one group of girls

> Make friends, make friends,
> Never, never break friends
> (children's chant from Opie and Opie 1959:324)

While Valerie Walkerdine noted the similarities between the prescriptive criteria of girlhood and those of feminine heterosexuality, she does not situate either girlhood or goodness in the contexts of class or race. Other writers argue that it is a *particular* classed and Anglo version of femininity which is constructed as the ideal type of pupil for all girls at school (Jones 1993; Kenway and Blackmore 1995).

The groups of white girls in my study related differently to the ideal type of girl pupil, and to the ideological imperative to be good. As we have noted, many of the girls (especially the middle-class girls) confirmed the criteria of goodness as central in their selection of a friend. Being disagreeable (bossy and openly assertive) was the exact antithesis of niceness. Pressures to *appear* compliant positively incited the subversive pleasures of committing disagreements to paper: Note writing materially assisted the task because it helped girls to avoid the damaging label 'horrid'. Erin's clique are discussing their preference for note writing:

Erin: Well if we say things out loud people will hear that we are having arguments and start picking on us.

Sam: . . . or the teacher will tell us off 'cos we're talking in lessons . . .

Saskia: . . . and it's safer to write notes sometimes. This morning we were writing notes . . . 'cos we want to go on a hack, a horse riding hack . . . 'em

VH: and they weren't spotted?

Saskia: No.

Erin: [disagreeing] Yes . . . the teacher came round, she looked at it, Saskia, but she didn't say anything.

VH: Have you seen . . . do boys pass notes?

Erin:
Saskia: } [in unison] No.
Sam:

VH: Why not?

Erin: They shout.

Saskia: Yeh . . . but we enjoy doing it more this way.

(Interview of Erin's clique, Eastford School 2nd year)

In participating in these clandestine cultural productions Erin and her friends were learning not only to constitute their feminine subjectivities in (conditions of surveillance) as specifically classed forms of niceness, they were also defining themselves against the noisier and messier form of boys' overt behaviours (Walkerdine 1985; Mac an Ghaill 1994) and at another level also learning about their ability to resist such surveillance.[1]

Correspondences: inscribing the proper identity of a middle-class girlfriend

By the time I began my detailed fieldwork with the class of 1S (see Chapter 3), the girls had already patterned themselves into distinct subdivisions within the class on the basis of perceived class differences which had been expressed through notions about differences of 'ability' and 'cleverness' (Arnot 1982). Erin's group consisted of Erin and Samantha (Sam) who formed the core relationship around which other relationships were predicated; Saskia, Anna and Tamara; Alexia, Olga and Clara. Saskia (according to her teacher) had always minded most about being positioned as outside the epicentre of the clique and compensated for this by having a brittle 'contingent' relationship with Anna (Davies 1984: 258). To complicate matters further, Anna described Saskia as her best friend (this same distinction is played out later between Anna and Natalie). Ms Spencer told me that Anna had originally tried to set up a network with Natalie and Laura, but an early misdemeanour involving truancy had resulted in Anna (lower middle-class) being 'warned off' the other two (black and working-class) as a 'bad lot', by her teachers and her mother.[2]

Erin's clan thus consisted of the strong core of Erin and her best friend Samantha, surrounded by a looser set of alliances. This patterning had taken shape within the first weeks at school. By the time I began observing the clique, their social negotiations appeared to have stabilized, but the initial imbalances and instabilities – so common in the early stages of girls' struggles to establish relationships – reasserted themselves and continued to condition how this clique conducted their friendship over three terms.[3]

At root was the dislocating effects of Saskia's affluence; more specifically it was the way she chose to manage her money that created endless problems within the clique's delicately poised system of friendship exchange. Her generosity, as the purveyor of endless sweets, treats and fad items, as well as her relentless social manipulations were acutely counter-productive – the former, because her largesse created resentment as her friends were unable to reciprocate, and the latter, because her mania for arranging things were construed as her being bossy and trying to buy friendship (see Griffiths 1995:85–8). The following account centres on exploring how Saskia's striving was read and resisted as bossiness.

If being good as a schoolgirl demanded the suppression of disagreements ('people will hear that we are having arguments and start picking on us'), then it was all the more important to invent a form of self-policing. I will focus upon three specific instances when Erin and her friends dealt with their disagreements through the ritual/regulation of a shared cultural code. The following detailed ethnographic account of what was in actuality endless hectic friendship transactions is traced (and to some extent fixed), through an analysis of their notes.

Saskia was the chief correspondent in her group because she was most interested in taking over its leadership. In the course of my time in Eastford I witnessed 50 or more note writing episodes and Saskia was the originator of 30 of them. Within these texts it is possible to encapsulate aspects of the story of Saskia's struggle as her friends countermanded her quest of popularity *as* power.[4] Given that this process took place throughout the course of the time I was in the field, I cannot for obvious reasons represent, indeed I was not privy to, all of the manoeuvres amongst the clique. I am compelled to condense the serial nature of their struggles into three key dramatic episodes; they all concern the girls' different abilities to command and demand inclusion and exclusion.

Issuing and accepting or rejecting invitations was a key social practice of Erin's clique. It was Erin's speciality and Saskia's passion. As other commentators have noted, the powers to include and exclude constitutes the currency of how girls variously negotiate their relations with each other (Llewellyn 1980; Nilan 1991). Saskia therefore sought to position herself as the group's main social manager but this was always a miscalculation and she was never granted the status she so desperately wanted. In interpreting the girls' practices I was reminded of Gilbert Osmond in the novel *Portrait of a Lady*; he was said to hold parties purely for the pleasure of excluding people (James 1987).

The use of the social resources of inclusion and exclusion within Erin's clique

Note episode 1[5]

It is important to bear in mind that the following note sequence covered only one day and included (in so far as it was possible to document) a 15 item exchange during a morning double history lesson and a subsequent 13 item exchange in the afternoon double general science lesson. All three main protagonists (Erin, Saskia, Samantha) took part in reading and writing the messages. These winged their way uninterrupted back and forth across the public space of the classroom. Girls' preoccupations did not interfere with their respective abilities to function formally, a finding which also says something about girls' skill in contriving their 'invisibility'. It is virtually impossible to conceive of boys being able, or indeed interested, in cooperating with each other in an equivalent cultural code.

Samantha was the main obstacle in Saskia's desire to become Erin's best friend. Saskia had to grasp any chances to outposition her. This opportunity optimally presented itself when Erin and Samantha fell out. In one such dispute Erin had then invited Saskia on a prestige trip to visit her father. Saskia, delighted by Erin's apparent interest in her, attempted to capitalize on the situation by issuing a counter-invitation to Erin (which specifically excluded Samantha) but this backfired since Erin had by then remade friends with Samantha.[6] The following is the initial sequence establishing the details of the respective invitations.

Saskia: I can invite one person to come to lunch because its only my brother in and he might not be in. Would you like to come for lunch? That way you can see the letter that my dad left, saying yes or no to [my] going with you.
PS. I am looking forward to this weekend.
Will I be staying the night at your dads?

Erin: You will be staying the night if we go on the coach journey to Bayside. But if we go somewhere else on the train you might or might not.

Saskia: Oh! I see. I hope we can go on the coach to the fair and seaside. But if we don't will we go to Bayside or Albion Towers or what?

Erin: I don't know yet. Would you still like to stay the night if we don't go to the beach?

Saskia: Yes, please. I'd *love* to.

The notes then go into other details about the journeys and Saskia writes back again with enthusiasm:

Saskia: It sounds great fun. I can't wait. But would you like to stay for lunch with me today.

Erin's reply is an unequivocal YES! Saskia moves at this point to exclude other girls from this special invitation:

Saskia: Okay but Sam, Olga and Anna can't come do you mind?

Erin: Yes, but I want to come. Why couldn't Sam eat with us at your house?

Saskia: Because I can only invite one person at a time because only my brother's in. Sorry. When there was four of us my mum killed me because of the mess and because I didn't tell her and my brother can't handle three, otherwise you know I would. Don't say I'm making up excuses its not nice.

I have been unable to track Erin's response but from the next communication, it appears that Erin decided not to go for lunch, due to pressure applied by Samantha. Saskia's action is to withdraw the offer:

Saskia: I am sorry but I can't invite you to my house whilst I feel guilty I'd like to talk it over with you but thanks to Sam I can't. If Sam decides that I am not making it up then maybe I won't feel so bad. But she has said things that make me feel so bad.

The main struggle concerned Saskia's effort to make Erin into her property. This could only be accomplished at the expense of two other girls – Samantha (who was Erin's best friend) and Anna, her own contingent friend. Saskia's insistence tested Erin, which she tried to resolve through negotiating Samantha's inclusion.

At first Saskia's motives and behaviour remained obscure to me. I thought her initiating energies (she seemed to be *the* one to hold parties, organize outings and manage arrangements) showed her *centrality* to the group and so indicated popularity. However, it became increasingly clear through her notes that she was always trying (and failing) to secure a popular following. She identified popularity with becoming Erin's best friend, but in desiring and not achieving this outcome she conceded rather than accumulated social power.

Conversely, Erin retains her dominance within the élite group. She has considerable social power to command because she is desired rather than desiring. She can enjoy testing her power over Samantha by positioning herself with Saskia. She had after all punished Samantha through making her jealous.

Saskia wants what Samantha has, namely the friendship of Erin and with that the associated social prestige. In trying to control access to Erin, Saskia was prepared both to jeopardize the relationship with Anna (who was effectively ditched as a result of her accepting Erin's invitation) as well as suffer the anger of Samantha. The outcome seemed to be the worst of all worlds, guilt and feeling bad. She was after all, at this point exposed – unable to claim Erin and yet shown to be cavalier in her treatment of Anna.

By the end of the day an unsteady truce prevailed. The following day, however, tensions within the group erupted again. The immediate provocation was Erin withdrawing her invitation to Saskia (re the trip with her father) and reissuing it to Anna. It was impossible to capture reasons for this change of mind. However this is less serious than it might be, because it is not the absolute empirical details of these manoeuvres that are my analytic focus, but their prevalence as an indicative practice of the economy of feminine forms of power.

Erin's tactics are as revealing as Saskia's about how their particular economy worked. Her moves show again that she had a complex investment in provoking the powerful positioning of herself as the subject of all three girls' attention (namely Samantha, Saskia and Anna).[7] Having the ability to command and control these emotions displayed (as well as ensured) that Erin was the most popular and most powerful girl within the clique. Erin's capricious (?) change of mind/heart provoked another crisis within the clique. Now it is Saskia's turn to be full of indignation.

Note episode 2

> *Saskia to Erin*: That's right blame it all on me why don't you. And Erin just because I took the note away doesn't mean to say that you shouldn't [be] my friend. But I don't care you take Anna on holiday with you and forget about me that's the best thing to do.

Erin denies this, insisting on her preference for taking Saskia.

> *Saskia to Erin*: Well I don't want to go with someone who doesn't look like they like me. You just go off with Anna and have a nice two days away.

This is somewhat ingenuous given Saskia's previous practice, a point not lost on Anna who eventually joined in the correspondence, demanding from Saskia an affirmation of her precise status:

> *Anna to Saskia*: If you don't want to be my best friend any more just say yes or no and get it over and done with because I'm not going to wait any more and don't think I'm going to go crawling back because I wont.
> From Anna.

Saskia's reply was equivocal. She simply scribbled, 'I don't know'. Anna then wrote back, 'That's fin[al]'. However, this wasn't the end. What appears to be at stake in these detailed (and apparently trivial) social dramas of intimacy are deeper meanings about belonging and striving for power and social prestige involving inevitable tensions over those girls deemed most popular. The girls in Erin's clique struggled with and against each other for the rest of the year. That they managed to keep the same personnel is intriguing. Anna and Saskia's relationship was in stasis as they both looked for other possible alliances but failed to secure them. They were therefore stuck with each other (Davies 1984).

In the second year things changed. Setting practices disrupted the élite clique's social groupings. In the process certain girls were detached from their previous alliances. Natalie had previously been close friends with Laura. Laura's demotion to a lower set meant that in certain subjects Natalie was 'friendless'. This caprice of differentiation strengthened Anna's resources and the two girls reconnected and became allies. Interestingly Anna characterized the relationship as casual, whilst Natalie claimed that they were best friends (see earlier).

The immediate context to the following episode is Saskia (yet again) excluding Anna from an arrangement in which the larger group would all meet at lunchtime at Samantha's house.[8] Her new exclusion generated a new series of notes. Below is a complete transcript of this crucial exchange.

Note episode 3

Anna/Natalie to Saskia: Saskia we are not your friend because you are a snide and you are not very nice.

Saskia to Anna/Natalie: I did not [rest of this obliterated]

Natalie to Saskia: because I am not
OK GOT THE MESSAGE

Saskia to Natalie/Anna: Why did Anna write the first one. Anyway I don't care what you say because words don't hurt. But I still like you both. Can't you answer.

Natalie/Anna to Saskia: Don't you come cheeky to me girl.

Saskia to Natalie/Anna: I'm allowed to say what I want to, it's a free world

Natalie to Saskia: Don't bubble up your mouth on me girl. Get it slag.

Saskia to Natalie/Anna: Why don't you try shutting up.

Saskia to Anna: Is Natalie my friend?

Natalie to Saskia: NO!

Saskia to Natalie/Anna: If NO you don't like me. Then I don't have to do anything you say. If you were my friend then I would but you're not so I won't.

	[A naturalistic, relatively neutral drawing of Anna]
Anna to Saskia:	If you must draw my wonderful complexion draw it properly
Natalie to Saskia:	But shut your mouth cheeky
Saskia to Natalie/Anna:	I know but I have never been good at art. PS. Is Nattie still my friend
Natalie to Saskia:	NO
Anna to Saskia:	A drawing of Saskia with sticky up hair – teenage style – with arrows pointing to her chest with the phrase 'Saskia Stevens' and 'flat as a pancake'[9]
Saskia to Anna/Natalie:	I don't care if that's what I look like. I like the hair cut though.

This note is one of the most elaborate that I collected. It has multiple discursive procedures. It contains both text and drawings which together orchestrate what has been called a 'discursive shift' (Rossiter 1994:4). Interestingly Rossiter's analysis of girls' drawings shows girls representing their 'failure' in the 'bad party' as being underlined by girls, for instance Mandy draws several examples of the awfulness of exclusion and isolation and being ignored. 'In both sets of drawings the accusation of failure comes from *other* girls' (Rossiter 1994:17, my emphasis). Rossiter understands this as girls acting like 'the projected judges of each other'. On the contrary, girls appropriate this discursive repertoire and then transform it into a specifically feminine social practice. The effectivity of girls' particular power to wound each other is precisely because such judgements emanate from one's imagined allies (girlfriends) as opposed to the enemy 'other' (boys).

In the earlier episodes Saskia and her friends write within the terms of 'bantering' (Milroy 1987) girl subjecthood, the social forms of which are referenced by the taken for granted common sense pleasures of girls' friendship in issuing and receiving invitations ('I can invite one person'; 'I am looking forward to this weekend'; 'Yes but I want to come'; 'I am excited about going').

However by episode 3 Saskia is no longer able to call upon these resources because she is compelled to participate in an altogether more grown up (?) sexualized discourse. She is drawn as a 'sight' of 'the male gaze' (Rossiter 1994:4) and made to appear through 'other eyes' as 'a slag' and 'flat chested'. Rossiter identifies this transformation with the specific social practice of an early adolescent mixed-sex dance party (Rossiter 1994). My material however, suggests that the capacity of girls to reposition other girls within the regime of the male gaze is a *general* capacity of girls' friendships.[10]

In terms of the particular sequence above, Anna, in alliance with Natalie,

constructs Saskia within the powerfully subordinating gaze of hegemonic (hetero)sexuality. In this episode the move takes place precisely
through an erasure of Saskia's identity as a subject of girlhood. This process is secured when she is 'objectified' after being made to dis/appear as
a girl child and re/appear as a sexualized object lacking in heterosexual
attractiveness.

The existence of the highly ritualized nature of the girls' exclusionary
practices indicates cultural resources deeply embedded in normative gendered ideologies which cut across relations of social class. We will meet
them again later (see Nilan 1991). Not only is Saskia now written off
as a 'snide', she is literally (and metaphorically) drawn within another
regime of meaning (of 'slag' and 'flat-chested') all the more effectively
to exclude her from the pleasures of girlhood and feminine approval.

Understandably, these responses produced very painful feelings. Saskia
gives explicit voice to her feelings in her earlier self-reflexive comment-
aries (See episodes 1 and 2). It is significant that she consistently tries
to redistribute social blame onto other girls: Samantha (for being jealous
and for not liking her, see earlier) and Erin (for excluding and for not
liking her).

The last sequence shows her attempting to resist by *denying* her feelings. She tries to generate a third discourse of individual rights (of free
speech for example). This is a bourgeois preoccupation (see Chapter 7
where other middle-class girls in my study speak about their 'rights') but
it is a weak position to make against the power of the stronger code of
girls' friendship and the all-pervasive force of the male gaze. Through
locating herself in the discourse of personal rights, she ultimately dis-
qualifies herself from claims on the loyalties of other girls.

She also struggles simultaneously to pull back the girl position by
attempting to neutralize the stronger discourse of heterosexuality (the
not being attractive enough discourse; Hollway 1984:240) through a
light touch of humour ('I don't care if that is what I look like. I like
the haircut though') but to no avail. Saskia's insistence on trying to
assume the social power of popularity/friendship without first meeting
the criteria of its ethical structure and practical manifestation left her
out of its very terms, 'If NO you don't like me. Then I don't have to do
anything you say. If you were my friend then I would but you're not
so I won't'.

Her persistent failure to honour co-dependencies was punished through
the production of guilt and isolation. Not only was she positioned outside of the discourse of girls' friendship, she was also practically and
effectively excluded from the group. She was ill for two weeks and in
fact never returned to the school.

Negotiating feminine friendship and its associated powers is a delicate
business, being always already constituted through the socially coercive

presence of the male gaze, which endlessly seeks to position girls within its regulation. We have seen that a key sanction to disqualify a girl from friendship is to relegate her from claims to femininity by implying that she looks insufficiently attractive. We will see the recurrence of this sanction again.

In examining the detailed workings of the early stages in the formation of relationships in one girls' group, we have seen something of what is at stake inside the culture of girls' friendship. Best friends are a specific feature of female relations (Llewellyn 1980; McRobbie and Garber 1980; Griffiths 1995). Best friendship represents in dramatic form the features found more diffusely within the wider networks and understandably the struggles around the role are usually the most acrimonious because this relationship is the most invested.

The desire to become and the fear of being displaced as a girl's significant other appears to be what Erin, Samantha, Saskia and Anna all bring to the negotiations. However, girls' tangible desires for power through friendship have to be reconciled with its ethical rules. These social rules are premised on the exact opposite of undisciplined individualism. My understanding of the ethical basis and ethical rules of female friendship confirms what other researchers have discovered (McRobbie 1978; McRobbie and Garber 1980; Nilan 1991; Griffiths 1995). The central premise of girls' friendship are: reliability, reciprocity, commitment, confidentiality, trust and sharing. The repertoire of emotions that are provoked if these rules are broken are as powerfully felt and as dramatic as those that have characteristically been claimed as the sole prerogative of sexualized relations (Coward 1986). Girls' 'divorces' are messy, as we can see in what happened to Saskia.[11]

One outcome of the pressure on girls to convert the wider loyalties of friendship into the exclusivities of best friendship is an implosion of individual power. It is not that girls in Erin's clique did not experience differential *feelings* of power through their ability to access other dimensions: being clever; being pretty; being good at games. They did. It is more that all of these other forms of cultural capital were incessantly evaluated within the domain of their friendships. Importantly therefore, in settling their alliances girls had to position themselves very carefully, lest their success in these other dimensions was perceived as disadvantaging one's peers (Davies 1984).

Equally, being thought 'bossy' could be the way in which highly ambitious girls are socialized into disguising their competence. After all Saskia's worst fault, condensed in the phrase 'showing off', placed her not only outside of the rules of social reciprocity, it also undermined her claims to be suitably 'nice' – as we have seen, a routinely invoked middle-class feminine form. As one of her friends cryptically remarked, 'She wasn't as nice as she was supposed to be'.

Notes

1 Interestingly few social researchers have spotted these notes and their significance. There are literally passing references to them in (Lever 1976:484; Davies 1984:258–60; Pollard 1984:242). My field logbook is one long litany of the girls' respective fall-outs, show-downs and pranks – all done more or less surreptitiously through their sending of notes or whispers. There are details of Anna and Saskia sharing a boyfriend and their teasing each other about him; testing each other about fancying other boys as well as commiserating about being asked out by certain boys; there are occurrences of Olga and Saskia falling out about supposed work partnerships; of a false love letter simulated by the girls and sent to Samantha, purporting to be from one of her admirers.

2 Deliberate interventions into the choice of friends recurs throughout the ethnography indicating the wider pressures being brought to bear upon how girls act even in their so-called private lives. For example Princess and Jude were originally close friends, but their equally bad exam results led Princess's mother to insist that they had to be separated (see Chapter 5) – but see how this is subsequently represented by the girls.

3 The way the girls in the élite group behaved provides an interesting point of comparison with the way Iris and Sonia performed their friendship. It is not simply that their friendship served the purpose of eliminating strife (though this was the case), it has something to do with their having far less to struggle over. Negotiations in Erin's clique were so tortuous as a result of them having so many distinctions to squabble over. It would seem, at least in terms of Iris and Sonia, that poverty speeded up the construction of their solidarity.

4 Girls had a distinct vocabulary for allocating moral judgements in the economy of popularity/unpopularity. Another girl told me the meaning of the following terms: 'skank': a girl who is unreliable, who makes arrangements and then fails to honour them; 'snide': a girl who is said to have told a confidence to someone else and/or who leaves the prior friend; 'user': probably the most painful term. It is often used in situations where one person has been popular and for some reason is made unpopular. This person then makes friends outside the group.

5 I've retained the term girls give to describe this form of communication.

6 As Lois, the 13-year-old daughter of one of my best friends expressed it, 'the best friend system hang[s] heavily at . . . school' and she goes on to characterize this culture amongst her class in the following terms: 'If your best friend isn't in school, you *ask* somebody else if you can go with them and their best friend. I think that the system of asking people is just a way of making sure that you don't invade a "best-friend's" space.'

7 Whilst becoming the object of three girls' desire is certainly a seductive position, it is also a predicament – a fact acknowledged by Erin in another note: 'I think if Saskia invites me and Olga to her house on Saturday then you can share me, but Saskia, it's up to you but you'd better invite someone else or two people will go off with each other and the other will be alone' (communication sequence 6, Item 10).

8 To prevent Anna from going, Saskia had taken it upon herself to tell Anna

that Samantha's mother would be there. In the event this was untrue and Erin's clique minus Anna met at Samantha's house. According to my interview with Anna, this hit her very hard since she had lost her other source of social support (Natalie, who had made other arrangements). Social isolation and 'leaving a friend' is considered a serious breach of social etiquette.

9   In the margins of this sequence was one other drawing of Saskia. It is of a large face with an open mouth. Intriguingly Jude broke with her previous close friend Princess through exactly the same tradition; she sent her what she described as a 'rude drawing' (see Chapter 5 for a critical reappraisal by Jude's current white friends of the nature of this cross-race relationship).

10   This discursive practice resonated with other practices I observed. Michelle, a new girl (1S) initially attached herself to the only other African-Caribbean girl in the class. However this upset the balance between Natalie and Laura; Michelle was eventually excluded through a similar (whispering) campaign during which both girls critiqued her body. This was contradictorily said to be 'baby-like' and 'out of control' (see Canaan 1986).

11   In a closing interview with Saskia before she left the school, I asked her to comment on the changes within her relationships. She spoke of coming back from her holidays and, as she put it, 'some really good friends . . . didn't want to know me anymore'. She spoke specifically about being shouted at in the street and also recalled in elaborate detail another rejection process: the same girls made 'anonymous' phone calls to her home and left messages on the telephone answering machine (pretending to be the household's ex-au pair). As part of this attack Saskia was also accused by one of her 'enemies' of calling her mother a 'slag'. It was at this point, according to Saskia, that Saskia's mother interrupted the anonymous phone calls to reprimand the caller. The complex cultural relays between inside/outside schooling can only be hinted at in this example. There is an impreciseness about the girls' identities but there is no confusion about the continuity of practices centring upon secrecy, sexuality and exclusion. The premediated campaign suggests that collective punishment is being meted out in no uncertain measure. In the same interview Saskia stated that, 'You don't really need *best* friends when you can have *good* friends', and optimistically anticipated her new (private) school through initial references to the 'warmth' and 'friendliness' of the girls, who she described as 'very nice'.

Chapter 5

CULTURAL PRACTICES OF FRIENDSHIP AMONGST WHITE WORKING-CLASS GIRLS

Introducing Jude's group: typical girls?

Judith (Jude) and her group of friends had been introduced to me at Crossfield School as 'typical'.[1] This term condensed two related meanings. On the one hand, it acknowledged their status as traditional products of a very familiar working-class culture (the school had until the mid-1980s recruited from a predominantly white community; many of the senior women teachers at the school had taught the girls' mothers) and on the other hand, 'typical' carried the subtext of a white ethnic identity.

However recent changes in local authority policy (the instituting of free bus passes) had transformed the school, because an increasing number of Muslim girls travelled in from the other side of the borough. The failure of the school, and the local authority, to confront the white girls' racist resistance to the changes to 'their' school was evident. The pupil groupings were to all intents and purposes socially divided into broad 'racial' lines – white and non-white. I shall never forget the time I went into a classroom during a pre-Christmas session, when the class was doing a quiz. There were two competing teams, one of white girls and one of Asian and African-Caribbean girls. The teacher did not appear to notice or if he did, elected not to intervene. During the course of my fieldwork several fifth year Asian pupils had gone to the senior staff to report the prevalence of racist abuse, but whilst individual members of staff were appalled by their stories and took individual action against the perpetrators, there were no whole school policies for managing the generalized racism of the school culture. Learning about Jude's friendship group uncovered clues about how this 'racialization' had taken place:

VH: How long does the history and development of your group go back?

Maureen: At this school really didn't it . . . Some people know us from the other [primary] school – that we got really got together.

Nina: We two [indicating Maureen] have known each other for 10 years. From infant school wan't it?

Gina: I've only been here a year.

Nina: I've known Judith for four years.

Maureen: I've never spoken to Judith for the first year because she used to go around with this black girl called Princess. She thought she was hard walking about.

VH: Who thought she was hard?

Maureen: Princess! She did! She gave Judith a bad image. I think. I didn't used to like her [to Judith], but now. . . . [inaudible] she's gorgeous . . . lovely.

VH: [to Maureen] When did you get to know Judith?

Maureen: When Princess and Jocelyn used to go around and then when Gina came to this school.

Gina: And I started to get friendly with Maureen. She was in my class and I started to go round with Judith. So we all started to go around together.

Maureen: With Frances [Frankie]. There were loads of us. About twelve. And now there's just us lot.

VH: Why did you split up?

Maureen: Because we chucked everyone else out we don't want.

When challenged to explain in more detail 'why [they] chucked every-one else out', the group members further developed the themes of race and reputation. Their version of the past produces Princess and Jocelyn as distinct enemy others.[2] Questions of race therefore were embedded in questions of who was, or who wasn't a friend. Drawing boundaries against these two girls (the former is African-Caribbean, the latter, her friend, a white working-class girl) involved racialized sexualization *as* denigra-tion. 'Hard' for example connotes two contrasting and gendered clusters of definitions. The attribution of Princess as hard was an elaborate echo of the girls' endless speculation about the 'hardness' of the African-Caribbean boys the girls knew. When applied to black boys it was a highly ambiguous term referencing an admired but troubling sexualized 'cool' style.[3] When applied to Princess it was a straightforward pejorative. As the object of fear and dislike, the white girls put her into the category of 'bad image', such as 'slag'.

Girls finding the 'Other' 'contaminating' recurs throughout my data (we have met it already – see p. 33; see later in this chapter). 'Othering'

organizes the social conditions under which these girls' friendships oper-
ate. The point is not that such judgements reflect 'reality'.[4] We are talking
about the discursive, as opposed to the real subject, but we note that
such attributions cause real pain, have real material and ideological effects
and code the interpersonal as a medium of power.

In conditions of surveillance, the place in heterosexuality Jude and
her friends were 'allowed' not only assumed a subordination to boys, it
also implied a subordination to a specific group or class – white boys.[5]
As Maureen explained to me:

> Once you've been out with a black bloke, you find that the white
> blokes don't really want to know . . . they don't like to think that
> they're sharing their woman with black blokes I suppose.

This assumption was widespread within her group. Another of the girls
told me that her brother had threatened to 'beat her up' if she ever came
home with a black boyfriend. Jude's group noticeably reserve their fier-
cest vitriol for white girls who they deem to have transgressed this racist
'honour code'. They call such girls 'wog meat', and 'black boy lover' (see
later). The girls come to see other white girls as sexual deviants since, as
they say, the white boys 'won't touch them any more' (see the 'bitching'
extract later). The force is not only that of compulsory heterosexuality
but compulsory white racist heterosexuality.

Maureen however, is particularly fascinated by black boys. Her talk
returns again and again to the 'hard, cool' African-Caribbean boys. She
speaks the most about 'blackness' in terms of evident attraction and endless fascination. But she cannot possibly own that desire. Instead she must
prove her whiteness by distancing herself from the 'Other':

> *Maureen*: If I didn't have all these friends I think I would crack up.
> *VH*:   What do you do when your best friend's away? Say there
>   was just Judith here and you four weren't here?
> *Sally*:   We'd just hang around with the Pakis. Wouldn't we?
> *Jude*:   I'd hate it, it's terrible.
> *Maureen*: I *don't*! I'd just sit on my *own*!

The boundaries are again defined through racist exclusions. If Sally
(and by implication anyone else) is to consider themselves as belonging
– being 'one of us' – then they patently cannot be seen with 'one of
them'. Maureen's role in establishing and mediating the group's (racist)
'common sense' is pivotal. Her vehement rejection of any alliance with
Asian or other non-white girls sets the framework of 'common sense',
within which any previous cross-racial social bonds are evaluated negat-
ively. The complex repositioning of Sally is a case in point.

Sally's comments expose her to the full force of Maureen's scrutiny.
Finding herself contradicted by Maureen, Sally goes to immense ideological

efforts to disassociate herself from her own remarks. She immediately uses the following exemplary story to reposition herself with the group by being against black and Asian girls:

Sally: I came to school once and not one of you was in at break. I just went out and at dinner time I just sat in the common room all by myself. There's so many – all the coloured people – stay in there and that. They just . . .

Jude: [sarcastically] Well you've got Princess or Jocelyn to talk to.

Sally: Yes, that's right . . . all my friends . . . [sarcastically laughing]. My little friends . . .

Maureen: [sardonically] Or the Asians.

The repositioning of Gina within the group was less apparent, but equally telling. Having been expelled from her previous (private) school Gina initially teamed up with Razia.[6] Gina however eventually qualified for membership of Jude's group through 'messing about' and 'having a laugh' (Woods 1977:178; Griffiths 1995). Gina 'confesses' this past:

Gina: I did [sit with the Asian girls] when I first came here.

Jude: [to me] Gina used to hang around with Razia.

Sally: Remember when Jocelyn used to hang around with Princess, remember that. I hated her. In the first year . . .

Jude: She's still the same now.[7]

Nina: She's a right snob.

Maureen: [returning to my original question] As long as there's two of us in we meet at break time and dinner time.

However, in accomplishing her place in Jude's group Gina was in danger, as her father used to beat her if she produced poor school work. Her failure to correctly negotiate the space between doing enough work to please her father, but not too much to alienate her friends, was revealed in an appalling irony. Jude told me that it was her friends who had noticed Gina's bruises and told the senior staff at the school. They notified social services, who interceded to warn her father.

Gina's recuperation within the white girls' group is secured, but Sally's desperate bid to belong is only partially successful. The ironic references to Princess and Jocelyn by Jude, and to 'the Asians' by Maureen and finally by Sally herself to 'my little friends' recognizes her liminality.

'Bitching': sexual contradictions and sexual competition

The friendship history of Jude's group thus persistently rearticulates the racist practices found in the local 'heterosexual market-place' (Griffin

1985). Indeed it was because the girls operated across the domains of friendship/schooling and the domains of courtship/dating that the ideologies of the latter was reactivated in the former and vice versa. As I have suggested in the opening chapters, the forms of femininity taken up in girls' friendships cannot be sequestered from how girls experience boys and masculinity. This was powerfully shown in the case of Gina and Jude by their co-membership of the mixed River Bridge gang.

Talking me through their complex relationship to the gang elicited a set of embedded distinctions which revealed the increasing sexualization of their involvement with individual boys. The move from belonging to one's girlfriends, to belonging to the mixed gang, to belonging to individual boys staged the girls' journey from girlhood to their status as (hetero)sexual girlfriends:

> *Jude*: Oh there used to be *tons and tons* of us . . . [recalling the gang]
> *VH*: Did you miss them? Do you miss this big group?
> *Gina*: No . . . not really . . . we did at first . . .
> *Jude*: We see them now and again and always say hello to them.
> *Gina*: I don't . . . I don't.
> *VH*: How long ago was that? When you were 13 and you're now 14?
> *Gina*: We just stopped going around with them a couple of months ago . . .
> *VH*: Did you? Why was that?

At this point both girls describe their particular individual relations to specific boys which signified their break from the wider gang:

> *Gina*: I started seeing Rickie and Jude started seeing Tim again.
> *VH*: Oh really. So you've been out with two boys from this group? Liam and Rickie [puzzled by new information which contradicted what the girls had told me earlier].
> *Jude*: [Explaining] She was going out with Liam, then she saw Rickie, and I went out with Tim and I got off with Greg and I got off with Gizmo [laughs] . . . [inaudible].

The girls patiently define the differences in circulation here:

> *VH*: I've still got to get this right . . . so there's 'getting off with'?
> *Jude*: Yeah, that means kissing 'em.
> *Gina*: [inaudible] kissing 'em.
> *Jude*: That's just the one night.
> *VH*: [mimes simple kiss]
> *Gina*: [laughs] Not exactly like that.
> *Jude*: Then there's 'seeing'.
> *VH*: 'Getting off with' and 'seeing'.
> *Jude*: Seeing a boy.

Gina: Seeing means there's no connection.
Jude: You're not 'going out with' each other, but you're not 'getting off with' each other, you're 'seeing each other' which [means] you can always get off with someone else.
Gina: If he wants . . . 'cos you're not tied.
Jude: Both of you can.
Gina: Both of you can.
VH: And three?
Jude: Going out with means . . .
Gina: You're totally committed [laughs].
Jude: You can't do nothing wrong otherwise you're finished. And then there's marriage [laughs]. Oh God!

The girls in Jude's group engaged in the pleasurable (and not so pleasurable) 'inevitability' of heterosexuality, completely aware of the possessive forms it takes. Their seduction by its promises and the status it conferred was confirmed despite their personal experiences of sexual and social coercion. They spoke in common sense terms about 'men wanting results' (that they were only after one thing) as well as expressing their awareness of the temptations of 'getting carried away' (Sally and Nina) and of 'turning them on but never letting them touch yer' (Jude). It was in short a (public) account of heterosexuality through which girls located the only possible place for themselves as its objects, rather than its subjects.

In the revised version of what Jude's group *now* stands for – a group of white non-snobs – those girls who did not prove themselves sufficiently 'white' and 'working class', that is 'non-boffin' and 'non-slaggy', could be, and were, marginalized. Significantly, sexual surveillance even undermined the alliances which made up Jude's group. Frankie and Maureen described Jude (for example) as having a 'bad name' using the mere fact of her being 'desired' as evidence, as they put it:

Frankie: And 'er Rickie wanted to go out with Judith, 'cos he wanted to give her one.
Maureen: So she must have had a bad name [quietly].

As we have already seen bitching was a major cultural practice of Jude's group. The pleasures it delivered and the pains inflicted derived from the girls' supervening investment in sexual and social competition, as opposed to feminine solidarity. Below we see a classic piece of bitching in which all these themes converge as Jude and Gina speak of the pleasures and power of being purportedly the only girls in the mixed River Bridge gang. They are referring (nostalgically) to the time prior to their move into the more advanced stage of heterosexual dating routines:

Jude: At one time there was only me and Gina going around with all the boys [giggle] and that was good, wasn't it, Gina?

Gina: Yeah, but . . . it was bad image, wasn't it? Over River Bridge, not image, but a bad reputation, didn't we?

Jude: I didn't go over there.

Gina: No, but . . . that time . . . the first time we went over . . .

VH: Because you were two girls and so many boys? Who gave you that image?

Gina: I don't know. J.W. told us, didn't she?

VH: And what was the bad image about?

Gina: I don't know, she never said . . . She just said, 'You're getting a reputation over there.' We only went over there once, didn't we?

VH: From who? The people who live there?

Jude: From the girls . . . the other girls, isn't it?

Gina: I think it was just . . . jealous really.

Jude: Jealous!

Gina: 'Cos there was a lot of good-looking boys there . . . wasn't there?

VH: Really?

Jude: We used to go around with a lot of good looking boys.

VH: Of these? This group here?[8]

Gina: We used to go down the road and no girl dare come up.

Jude: I mean the boys used to come up and put their arms round us like a mate . . . they used to come up and say 'All right Jude', 'All right Gina', like that and put their arms round us and we didn't even get one dirty look . . . No girl dare even blink at us.

VH: Why?

Jude: I . . . [laughs] we'd do 'em over wouldn't we Gina?

The ideological loop has come full circle. Jude and Gina construct a privileged place for themselves as chosen girls in the gang but such power is also conditional – their 'reputations' are on the line. Other girls are to blame – their competitors and rivals for the power which flows from being in among the boys in the gang. The difficulty of claiming a public identity as being sexually active coerces girls into finding a 'nice' boy and into proclaiming romanticized forms of social and sexual behaviour. After this point, their talk shifts properly into what I interpret as their well-rehearsed verbal game – bitching.

Having claimed that the gang contained just a couple of girls (apart from them) they then produced a mantra about every other girl from the River Bridge gang:

Jude: But they were a bunch of idiots anyway. Weren't they?

Gina: They'd been out with every one of them.

Jude: Every single one of them!

VH: Who [were] was this . . . [inaudible].

Jude: The girls? Candy – and she's the . . . She's the biggest . . . She's been to bed with every one of them.

Gina: Every single one of them!

VH: Who said . . . who said that?

Jude: Oh she admits it! She's not shy about it!

Gina: Or embarrassed.

Jude: She's proud of it.

Gina: And she's nothing to look at . . . she's enormous.

Jude: Ugly, fat cow.

Gina: And she wears . . . wears the most . . .

Jude: Horrible clothes.

Gina: To make her look bigger.

Jude: Yes . . . she wears big, baggy clothes to make her look bigger.

Gina: And there's Lynn and she's short and stubby.

Jude: A tart . . . [giggles]

Gina: Yes . . . I tell you she put . . .

Jude: Plastered in make-up.

Gina: One inch foundation on, let it dry and put another layer on . . . she's caked her make-up on. There was Louisa, she's cross-eyed and buck teeth . . . She used to think herself lovely.

Jude: She looks pretty if she didn't have cross-eyed and buck teeth. She'd be quite all right.

Gina: And she used to go shoplifting from BHS.

Jude: I know! Nick her knickers from BHS [laughs].

Gina: She used to nick 16 pairs of knickers at one time!

Jude: From BHS [laughs]. And there's Bobo . . .

Gina: Yeah Bonnie, just put Bonn.

Jude: She was a Paki lover [laughs conspiratorially].

Gina: Yes . . . she went out with a Paki.

Jude: [giggles] Lorraine went out with blacks.

Gina: Lorraine?

Jude: Yeah, Lorrie . . . Lorrie V.

Gina: She went out with all black boys.

Here we are back on the same terrain of the co-constructions of class, gender and race as 'common sense' properties of the girls' cultural understandings about sexual and social boundaries. Here are heterosexual prescriptions about who it is permissible to be seen with – and who it is definitely not.

In this economy, the incentive of 'othering' was enormous – how else could you claim to be normal, acceptably attractive and OK? It is all those other girls who can be made to carry the 'bad' bits of femininity – active heterosexual desire is something only other girls act upon. These social positions and competitive hostilities carry enormous social, emotional and psychological compulsions because they constituted how Jude and Gina come to resolve *who they are.*

Paul Willis's work (1977) offers a model of cultural production and re-production which suggests some insight into the above processes. Mascu-linity is classed through the lads' own cultures, through social processes whereby the 'lads' perpetuate themselves as the macho workers of hard industrial (as opposed to mental) labour. They are said to construct a set of identifications which more successfully inscribes them in capitalist class relations than imposed dominations. Similarly Jude and Gina elect to read themselves in competitive relations with other girls – to become 'bitches' because their investment in the heterosexual marketplace is seen as the only route through to what they see as desirable femininity. Here are moments in the elaboration of what Willis identifies as girls' 'own vital power' which he locates as 'applicable not to "work" and "industry" but to complex and contradictory sexual manipulation' (Willis 1977:153).

Willis's 'lads' discounted mental labour because of its pre-existent dis-cursive association with despised femininity. Jude's group pathologize feminine differences to secure for themselves an imaginary place as appro-priately (hetero)sexual. However they are ultimately unable to transcend the surveillance of reputation. After all even their own discourse tells them as much: 'It was bad image wasn't it?' Their bitching is a measure of these contradictions.

From here to obscurity: being one of the girls

As Willis's argument implies, working-class girls' investment in hetero-sexuality was in part mandated by their disinvestment in schooling as a source of (academic) prestige. Jude and her friends' resistance to the demands of school took the form of their opposition to cleverness/stu-diousness, which as we have seen took an invariably social form. If part of the pleasure of Willis's 'lads' was about being anti-social – 'bad, mad and dangerous to know' – then Judith and her clique preferred more subdued and subtler forms of opposition. They had, along with many girls in both schools, a *laissez-faire* attitude to school attendance. As I wrote in my field notes, 'A sort of take it or leave it, with an emphasis on the "leave it"'. They were seldom openly hostile to teachers only becoming so if the staff were too keen in their pursuit of the "disappeared".' It was a stance with which many of their mothers colluded, sometimes using their daughters for a range of social services, child care supervision and domestic duties. Nina's mother for example demanded her company for a hospital appointment, 'because she was lonely'.

Their reaction to school was not so much the product of antagonism, but rather the end result of the girls' inveterate antipathy to being thought a snob. Snobs were people who were 'lonely' and incapable of appropriating school through its most important dimension – that of the social. Jude's group thus constructed most of the content of school as 'boring'. They would take every opportunity to convert the inertness of school into a chance to do their friendship work. One strategy was note writing because here their knowledge of, and fascination with, the personal was allowed its own space beneath the surface, as part of the 'unofficial' curriculum:

VH: Can you remember in the first or second year – did you ever send notes to each other?

All: Yes!

Sally: Yes, me and Gina were doing it today 'cos I got told off for her speaking.

Gina: I was not speaking – I pulled the book down like that [miming] and you said, 'Cow, put it up here'. Miss Hunter said, 'Sally', and I said, 'Wot! I ain't saying nowt'.

VH: What are these notes about then?

Nina: Me and Jude used to write 'What did you do at the weekend?' and things like that.

Jude: I've pages at home from all of us. I've got a little cupboard filled with letters we've sent to each other. It's so funny. Full of rough books.

They had other resources too. They would hold team talks at break at their rendezvous point (always the same location), and checked out each other's action plans for the day. Sometimes an active dislike of one particular teacher prompted a bunk, sometimes it was just nice weather, making the park an attractive option. Occasionally someone elected to skive for fear of reprisals for unfinished homework. Sometimes it was jointly done by them all just for the hell of it, because they had their own urgent business to attend to. This was particularly the case when boyfriends were giving them trouble. These break or lunch time meetings would often overrun the allotted time so if it could be managed, they adjourned to a nearby house.

Judith (like Carol, see Chapter 6) operated a timetable determined by their social needs as opposed to the one organized by academic demands. Her teachers commented to me that they had never seen her at school so often (this was during the time when I shadowed her for a week). She actually liked most of her teachers. They in turn liked her, but these personal affiliations were never in themselves sufficient to undermine her resolve not to break faith with her group and their class-specific experience of being 'one of the girls'.

VH: If you've got these plans like for a career, what part does school play in it, like getting you from where you are now to where you want to be?

Gina: The way we look at it now... it's too late [giggles].

Jude: It is too late [emphatically].

VH: You reckon?

Gina: We should have grafted from the third year. I mean you can mess about in the first, second, year but you've got to get down to it in the third year.

VH: So you think you've blown it at school?

Gina: I think I have anyway.

Jude: No way I'm going to pass that French exam. We're not going to pass any of them. We don't do maths, do we?

Gina: We go to the lesson but we don't do it. And he doesn't make us.

VH: You don't do it. What do you do then?

Gina: Talk.

Jude: We just sit there and talk.

Not 'settling down to work' was fundamental to the maintenance of their friendship. Jude said that those who work only do so "cos they've got no other friends'. Gina held a more ambiguous view, derived from pressure exerted at home for her to do well (see earlier). Gina contests the orthodoxy, attempting to construct bunking as a sign of immaturity:

Gina: We are immature because we won't work and we've got our exams coming up.

Jude: That's not immaturity Gina, 'cos we don't want to work!

Gina: Yes it is! Because I mean we talk about having a good job and that and having a flat and that... when we leave school.[9]

Jude: Yeah but, just because we don't pass our French exam or our maths exam doesn't mean to say we're not going to get a flat or anything when we leave school or get a job.

Gina: Judith, if we don't get any exams we aren't going to get a job.

Despite what might seem to be the compelling logic of Gina's argument (the voice of Gina's father as the policeman in the head is heard throughout, a highly specific instance of ventriloquism; see Bakhtin 1981), Judith refuses to acknowledge their preference for friends over work as being either 'stupid' or 'immature'. She neatly inverts the argument:

Jude: Yeah, but why go to lessons if you know you don't have to go. If you know you don't really wanna go.

Gina: But that's why we don't go, 'cos we know we can get away with it.

Jude: Yeah, but we're not immature then are we? We're sensible!
Gina: Yeah [sighs].

Gina still finds this hard to reconcile to her own split feelings until Judith reminds her of her complicity in their joint opt out:

Jude: No, you're being stupid if you go to a lesson if you know you can get away with bunking it. That is being bloody stupid.
Gina: Why bunk it? Why bunk it?
Jude: 'Cos you have to sit in there and do the work. Now why bother doing the work if you know you don't have to?
Gina: You're being sensible if you sit in school and do the work.
Jude: Yeah, but why don't you then? Why don't you sit and do all the work if you want to be sensible?
Gina: I don't wanna.
Jude: Well, there you go then, you're stupid and you're [inaudible].
Gina: Yeah, I'm stupid and I know I'm stupid! [with resignation]

Whilst both defend their 'talking about something really interesting' because it confirms a particular role as each other's best friend, they nevertheless, as their discussion makes clear, express differences. In particular the social identity of 'immaturity' presents them with a dilemma. The complexities have two interrelated sources: the specific pressure Gina is under to 'be sensible' and their awareness that immaturity compromises femininity (Hudson 1984). If they are to reconcile their differences and confirm their friendship they are left with no option but to embrace the position of 'stupidity', as Judith tellingly asserts:

Jude: Yeah, but you like being stupid. Don't ya? [giggles]
Gina: Like everybody else does! [giggles]

'Coming out a lesbian': locating a transgressive text of female friendship

As we have seen when the girls in Jude's group sought out forms of social power they did so through negotiating two main trajectories: dimensions associated with becoming a girl's friend (being in Tamara's phrase a 'chosen girl') prior to the 'real' business of becoming a heterosexual girlfriend. Like all the girls in the study, they knew the rules about sexuality. As Amelia told me, 'If you go to a mixed school right, and you fancy few people like, but if you go to a girls' school right, you have to start fancying girls 'cos all you see is girls'. Gabbie in the same interview confirmed, 'I was meant to go to a girls' school right, and I changed it to Eastford School in case I come out a lesbian'. Presumably going to an all girls' school exerted its own additional pressures.

The following episode explores aspects of how Jude and Sally construct a playful escape from this 'heterosexual imperative' (Wilton 1993). For a fragmentary interlude the girls move into what Scheurich (1995: 246) has called 'chaos/freedom' – an instance allowing them to disturb the wearisome compulsions of 'normality'.

Their note came to my attention just prior to leaving the field, when I asked all the girls if they had any notes which they wouldn't mind my looking at. In response, Jude produced the following, which was written when she was in the third form. I have discussed it elsewhere under the category of 'transgression' (Hey 1995a, 1995b). It is an extremely interesting note, dense with dizzying discursive switches. It is edited because of space restrictions. The original has 39 separate exchanges.

'Girls' dirty writing': a social exploration of subversion/re/version

The main themes explored by Jude and Sally concern sexual identity, sexual practices and sexual desire. The document starts straightforwardly enough; Jude writes:

> Thanks for letting me have tea and that round your house tomorrow night. It should be good. Is it okayed with your mum? What did she say?
> Love Jude.

Sally replies:

> Dear Jude
> I haven't told my mum yet but she always lets me so I'll ring you up tonight about half past six to tell you but I know she will let you. Tomorrow night should be a laugh. Stuart will come with us though, okay?
> Love Sally

Sally indicates that she hasn't yet cleared it with her mother but anticipates no problem. She also informs Jude in tentative mode 'that Stuart will come with us though, okay?' The 'okay?' expresses an anxiety about the acceptability of the boyfriend to Jude. The girls had just started seeing boys.

Jude asks in return:

> What about Paul O will he be there? If he is, when you want to get off with him I'll distract Stuart and say you've gone to the toilet.

Jude enters the discourse of 'taking the piss out of boy/friends' with the mention of Paul. This discourse essentially parodies (masculine? macho?)

sexual appetites and predatoriness, since both girls play the part of sexual actors who represent each other as duping boys.

Sally to Jude:

I don't think he will be there but if he is thanks a lot. If you talk to Stuart I'll go outside and get away with Paul.

Jude to Sally:

Too right. I'd do the fuck'n same

The elaboration of an ironic 'common-sense' rationale follows:

Sally to Jude:

Well you only live once so why don't you enjoy yourself

This is instantly parodied and sabotaged through the humorous putdown:

Jude to Sally:

The scientifict [*sic*] proof shows that you can live twice so how do you feel?
Gutted.

Sally joins in through a combative rebuttal but then shifts the grounds of the discourse abruptly by taking up the position of the pupil:

Sally to Jude:

No not really because the scientifict proof shows that you can live three times if you like. So how do you feel? Gutted. By the way I didn't know how to spell scientifict so I copied yours.

Jude to Sally:

Mine is probably wrong too

The consolations of ineptitude are short lived as Sally returns to continue the more 'adult' transgressive verbal game:

Sally to Jude:

So why fucking write it.

Jude to Sally:

Because I pissen [*sic*] well did you prick with ears.

Now Sally tries to put Jude back into the 'pupil/child' place:

Jude – pissen is spelt pissing okay

Other commentators have noted how young girls adopt the 'teacher' position as a site of power (Walkerdine 1981). In this note the girls are not so much adopting it as parodying it, as their discourse about 'sex' takes place both under and beneath the teacher gaze. The shared frisson of subverting the power of others (masculinity/adult/teacher authority) is captured as they contrive their illicit sexualized girls' talk, conscious of, but defying the powerful excluded others. Through their incessant references to each other as pupils, they pleasurably remind themselves that whilst they are physically controlled under the terms of institutional authority, they are simultaneously (if momentarily) outside of the official gaze. Hence they become more 'teacherly' *through* their scatology. Their most provocative and heterosexualizing comments emerge most forcefully at precisely the same time that they repeat the deadly redundant knowledges beloved of their teachers (the names of the planets). Their talk slides towards increasing levels of transgression, involving mouths and male and female bodies! They achieve this through neatly reappropriating official lesson content for their own subversive ends. Jude jokes:

Well you could fit all the planets in the world. That's Mars, Venus, Mercury, Pluto, Saturn, the Moon and the Sun.

At this point the topic of 'bodies' meets the 'theme' of 'sex talk'. Sally responds:

anyway they are 9 planets in the Universe so they would fit in your mouth not mine so shut up. Anyway I know what would fit in your mouth and that is a nice juicy prick.

Jude writes:

But how do you know?

Then follows a sequence about Paul's 'body' which leads to jokes about 'getting one's knickers in a twist' which then provokes an invitation to try lesbian oral sex. Sally responds to Jude's remarks:

Yeah, I like a little bit of both. Know what I mean?

It is as if having confronted the great unspoken about heterosexuality – that is, male bodies – they were empowered to examine the silenced aspects of their own sexuality and sexual desire. The girls puzzle about the meanings of their intimacy. Jude writes to Sally:

Well that's fine with me just as long as you don't pick on me. I mean you can pick on Princess or Jocelyn because I think they're a bit like that. They never let go of each other. Mind you the way we go on kissing each other on the cheek, people give us funny looks.

But they do not sustain this ambiguity for long, as shown by Sally's response:

Well, there's nothing wrong with that. We all know we like boys and that's as far as it goes.

Their textual flirtation with the lesbian positioning is managed by swiftly projecting the deviant possibilities onto others. Again the metaphors of space are important. It is the other girls (Princess and Jocelyn) who are 'the other side of the hill'. There is a narrative closure at the exact moment when both girls claim for themselves the position of heterosexuality and the more ambiguous sexual identity for Princess and Jocelyn. Jude signs off:

I know as long as we know that [i.e. that we only like boys], that's ok but I'm not so sure about Princess and Jocelyn you know.

What we have here I think is evidence of girls' anarchic questioning about normality which involves them in cultural efforts that momentarily destabilizes the category of white working-class femininity. We also have further indications that girls' presumed passivity as schoolgirls masks a great deal of cultural activity (the analogy with Gina doing stuff behind her book is instructive).

However, I am under no illusions that discursive subversions translate directly into actual sexual practices. Neither am I claiming that their 'sex talk' is liberatory. Such an argument would be unsustainable in the context of what we have already seen of the sexual politics of their relationships. However, the dimensions of play, escape and resistance shown here suggest domains of 'chaos/freedom' (Scheurich 1995) which should serve the function of provoking further speculations about other sites and forms of girls' practices within schooling.

Coming to inconclusions

This chapter has argued on the basis of some case study material that Jude and her friends had invested important forms of subjectivity in their own network. Their complex and contested alliances represented a resourceful attempt to hold together forms of social status and sexual identifications in conditions of masculine and adult surveillance. Jude and her friends knew the value of their status as sexy but not actively sexual girls. They sought a constant equilibrium in the racialized heterosexual marketplace and their best friendships provided forms of cultural capital, common sense evaluations which mediated their excursions there.

Their own friendship culture provided meanings about the right way to be through positioning the ideal friend as white, non-boffin, and not 'slaggy'. Their investment in that position was at the expense of other girls' social and discursive exclusions. As we have seen they could only produce themselves as occupying dominating positions within hegemonic racialized heterosexuality through taking up and redistributing sexual and racial identifications amongst 'other' girls.

Girls like Jude and her typical group loved each other as friends (and hated others as enemies), but they did not invest the same degree of emotion in their schools. Given the compulsions such practices expressed and employ, we should not be surprised that when 'typical' girls like Jude come to understand themselves, they do so through their friendship values and ideologies rather than academic evaluations.

This we could see in how they converted the sociability of each other into a form of oppositional, subversive and parallel set of meanings through which they took apart the official discourse. For Jude, making out at school was less about aspiring to futures proposed by adult middle-class values than about making out as one of the girls. Being a 'mate', in contrast, provided a vibrant form of feminine social identity that was seen as much more consonant with the world beyond school.

We have witnessed how Jude's group used their female friends in complex ways: to negotiate heterosexuality; to discover the 'right' way to be feminine – to be 'lovely, gorgeous' without being 'slaggy'; to be provocative without 'doing it'; as one of them memorably put it, 'to turn them on but not get carried away'. We have also seen how the familial and community basis to their racism policed not only the boundary between 'their girls' and black boys but also between white and black girls.

The interviews were also social events which provided yet another opportunity for the group to construct its specific version of cultural hegemony.[10] The practices which reaffirmed their 'typicality' also co-constructed class, gender and racialized meanings through their endless evaluation of those 'other' girls. These are lived moments when the girls recirculated and inflected cultural appropriations from their own working-class communities to reveal what I understand by the social practice of 'ventriloquism' (see Bakhtin 1981; Wertsch 1991, especially Chapter 8).

The material shows the force of an effective racist and class mandated form of social control working within this particular group of close friends. I have also suggested the means by which in certain circumstances, the same highly policed girls can acknowledge other needs – another discourse of desire, even if finally the girls draw the line to take their place as 'one of the girls'.

Notes

1 See Griffin (1985) for a gendered deconstruction of this term.

2 They did this through a series of exemplary retells, introduced by the phrase 'Do you remember?'. This strategy produces from all the discussants the required negative memories about Princess and Jocelyn. Accordingly, they were characterized as 'mouthy' (Jude and Maureen), 'difficult' (Maureen and Sally) and 'skanks' (Jude). They effectively reconstructed the exclusion.

3 Jude and her group used to go off site in summer to visit a group of boys from the nearby boys' school. They had formed friendships with African-Caribbean boys from this group. The way most of the girls talked about black boys was infused with the girls' tabooed but evident attraction to the myth of the black super stud (Segal 1990:175–81; hooks 1992:21–39). The eroticization of the forbidden has of course, historically structured white racist relations with black people (Segal 1990; hooks 1992).

4 Different 'reputation' terms figure in the repertoire of girls' attributive and evaluative languages according to the variable nature of the context. Princess's reputation was later attacked through the category of lesbian. See the discussion below.

5 The girls spoke endlessly about how to manage the politics of sexual access. Boys were 'only after one thing' and if the 'thing' they were after was them, it is not surprising that a vast amount of the girls' time was devoted to finding a 'nice genuine' boy and policing each others' reputations.

6 The social class position of Gina was complex. Her father held aspirational views about himself and his family. Forms of his proprietorial attitude are discussed later. Gina's move to a state school signified to him downward mobility. This is specifically alluded to in a later interview (see Hey 1988).

7 Jude is anticipating the point about Razia being a 'snob'.

8 I had been making a list of the boys' names in the gang.

9 Jude and Gina had said on another occasion of their plans: Judith wanted to work at the airport, whilst Gina wanted to work for a local hi-tech firm because 'they have company cars'. These ambitions also involved them leaving home and setting up a flat together (see Carol and Liz, Chapter 6). This escape motif is a very common working-class fantasy, even more fantastic given London's housing prices. Norma Sherratt has a thoughtful account of the way the ideology of glamour, which is attached to certain female jobs (usually to disguise their menial, poorly paid, low status), works to mediate the difficulties which girls experience in managing the struggle to achieve without jeopardizing their femininity (Sherratt 1983). She argues that glamour allows girls to retain their hopes whilst making the necessary adjustments to the difficulties of achieving their ambitions. She specifically identifies it as an ideological category which connects to an unconscious fantasy of escapism (see Skeggs 1994).

10 Jude's clique showed the effects of sharing this history in numerous ways. Technically it was difficult to transcribe my group interviews with them. They frequently spoke at once, finished each other's sentences, spoke in code and frequently told each other what they must think! Their mutuality encoded the group's 'common sense' and it was the prime medium for elaborating

and consolidating their identities. To the extent that I accepted them as they were, I too was also implicated in making their 'common sense'. By refusing the place of critic I was/am aware how complicity is to some extent *always* at stake in ethnographic practices. In making my decision to become one of the girls I retained the capacity to collect *how* the construction of race/ sexuality/class and gender presumes the conspiracy of belonging. I did not take up critical positions in relation to middle-class girls' classism either (see later).

Chapter 6

'HYPER FEMININITY REVISITED': A WORKING-CLASS GIRL'S HETEROSEXUAL EDUCATION

Introduction: 'Getting to know you, getting to know all about you?' – text and subtext in ethnographic field relations

My first meeting with Carol was when I almost bumped into her after a circuit run at Eastford with the fourth year girls. She had skilfully avoided the above exertion (confiding in me later that she had staged an injury). I didn't realize at the time that posing was one of Carol's typical cultural games. This only emerged when she became my 'minder'. Sharing Carol's company involved witnessing (as well as ineluctably becoming part of) her tendency towards self-dramatization. The following 'smashing her face' episode was typical.

Amy (one of her friends) had 'grassed', implicating Carol in the contraband circulation of cigarettes. Senior staff had tracked down the source of the supply, using the interrogation of Amy to provide substantive proof of Carol's involvement. Carol was ostensibly 'furious' about this, threatening Amy with dire consequences. She went in hot-blooded pursuit of the 'enemy' and I tagged along. I joined in the delegation headed towards the park, anticipating at least a verbally violent showdown. I did not have time to prepare my response if actual blood was spilled.

In the event, I needn't have worried; the clash was no more than a highly stylized dialogue. Amy defended herself against Carol's questioning and the situation was resolved when Carol claimed her moral victory because she (Amy) had 'taken the blame'. What had been billed as the female version of *Godzilla meets the Smog Monster* thankfully turned out to resemble no more than ritual posturing. Later in the week, when I asked about the event, Carol retorted, 'I nearly smashed her face in!'

The narrative of Amy 'getting smashed' was only one of the many non-events through which Carol lived her relation to me and to the world. It didn't matter to her that I'd actually witnessed the 'real' showdown. Carol was far more invested in transforming herself into the heroine of her own life (and this ethnography), than complying with the convention of documentary accuracy.

Carol took it upon herself to become my key sponsor at Eastford. She introduced me to several fourth year networks of working-class girls, in particular those who, like her, truanted a great deal. She was quite an expert in girlfriend knowledge, which was paradoxical since she herself subverted all the conditions considered necessary for doing friendship.

One important distinction, which Carol shared with those girls she called her friends, was the fluidity and contingency with which they formed and reformed their pragmatic alliances. Like other similarly dis-affected fourth years, she operated a set of serial relationships which she appeared to swap as regularly as her 'boyfriends'.[1] As O'Connor (1992) argues, girls/women need a material base in order to make and sustain their friendships.

Nevertheless the girls had developed a support network of sorts, even if it lacked the emotional intensity associated with best-friendship. For example, the problem of isolated girls was managed through the tactic of their acting as each other's minders when the regular friend was away. Carol, for example, took responsibility to look after Rita on several occasions when Liz was away: 'Carol is with Rita today, who she describes as "nervous and alone, since her friend won't be in until tomorrow", therefore Carol, has sort of "adopted" her' (field notes, 2:8).

There were other senses too, in which Carol minded girls which ex-pressed her expertise as a 'mother'. Carol's criteria of doing friendship derived more from concerns about girls' lapses in acceptably feminine self-presentation, than from expressions of social intimacy. She showed particular interest in Mary, who she had bluntly described to me as 'looking like a tramp': 'C going to help out by passing on her old skirts. It seems M's mum very controlling of M via control of money, i.e. no new clothes and in the household, won't let M use an iron. C took it as "common-sense" that appearance mattered' (field notes, 5/6).

I speculated that perhaps she too had become (like me) more of an observer of these relationships because she positioned herself outside of their controlling surveillance. As one of her acquaintances explained to me, she was not really popular with her male class peers because 'no one really knew her'. This is hardly surprising. She seldom put in a full week. When she did come to school, she only visited those lessons where she liked the teacher (like Jude and her friends in Crossfield).

Researching into Carol's life at school involved exploring the delic-ate themes of sexual and social identity. Furthermore, proposing their

interpretation also raises complex process issues about the social relations of ethnography; the ethics of participant observation; 'truth' and
substantive issues to do with problematic forms of social power for
working-class girls.

'Editing' Carol has involved making decisions about which parts of
her life to represent, since converting her into an academic artefact has
necessarily involved moving across the borders between the public and
the private (see the discussion in Chapter 3), and transfiguring a real
person into terms within my argument.[2] In choosing to assemble a story
from many sources, some of which were controlled by Carol (her retells and stories) and others which were not (the incidents which un-
folded before the pair of us during the course of quite intensive field
participant observations), one is involved in a reading which sets in context Carol's claims to a self-dramatized successful negotiation of heterosexual desire and subsequent claims to its associated forms of power
(see later).

Somewhat more complexly and unconsciously, my analysis also reflects
my own memories of being a different sort of working-class schoolgirl.
Carol's story therefore is not only built through my recontextualization
of aspects of her own representations of herself, it is also mandated by
intersubjective forces – of memories of growing up with and *against* girls
like Carol (see Chapter 2). In fact it was only in rereading the original
manuscript that I became aware that I had chosen the name of one of
my former best friends as her pseudonym!

My intention in claiming resonances between an ethnographic text
and aspects of my biography is not to stake a privileged claim on truth.
Rather it is to recognize the significant (if immeasurable) effects of personal history. The practice of re/membering has been surprisingly emotional. It has involved painful as well as pleasurable recollections (see
Thorne 1993). In getting to know Carol and other schoolgirls I have been
continually reminded of resonances from my own girlhood. At a deeper
level it is, however, 'difference' that constructs our relation and relationship and my rendition of it.[3]

In particular, the fact that I am telling Carol's story rather than she
telling mine, dramatizes the prevailing class and age relations between
us – which no amount of empathy or feminist commitment or sharing of the project can dissolve. The ability to tell another's story is a
concrete social practice of power and it crystallizes for me the distance
travelled out of my culture of origin. I both grew up with 'Carols' and grew
apart from and against them. Carol self-consciously mimicked the differences between us in the last days in the field at Eastford – she followed *me* around pretending to write her observations into a book!
The 'text' of Carol emerges out of the uneven interplay of all of these
factors.[4]

Sponsors and refuseniks: paradoxes and participations

Carol was positioned by school as a particular sort of girl. As the eldest girl in a large family living on supplementary benefit, she was described as a 'no-hoper' with 'problems' from a 'disadvantaged' background. She often described her family through the jobs she had to do – her mother had seven other children living at home as well as a third husband. She invariably produced herself as fighting back against perpetual familial and social control. Her mother called her a 'bad girl'. Her girlfriends called her 'larrupy' (loud-mouthed; see Jude's group depiction of Princess, p. 85, note 2).

This chapter documents how she strove to 'rework' her subordination as a working-class 'skivvy' by transforming herself into a heterosexualized 'proper young woman' – a strategy which she understood as the route to forms of power, pleasure and excitement unavailable at school and at home.

Having little stake in the sources of status and privilege promised through conforming as a 'good girl', she made herself into a star in the drama of heterosexuality, through a cultural investment in 'glamour' (Sherratt 1983) or 'hyper femininity' (McRobbie 1978; Connell 1987). Her most substantial assets in accessing this heterosexual economy was her body and her sense of self as 'sexy': 'Carol told me she was "proud" of her nickname of "Big Tits" though she remarked that she minded about the tone within which it was said' (field notes).

She constantly drew attention to her body in highly positive terms which is in complete contradiction to other girls' self-descriptions (see Chapter 7). She did so through comparing herself favourably to other girls, commenting upon other young women that 'they're a bit skinny up top'.[5] She did not fit the portrayal of an alienated pubescent girl (Simmons and Blyth 1987). Carol was neither self-conscious nor suffering from lack of self-esteem. Her reaction to the unhelpful coalition of the compulsions of schooling, bodily maturation, and the attractions of dating was to rationalize these contradictions by refusing to be positioned as a schoolgirl (Rossiter 1994; McRobbie 1978).

Carol's negotiations of bodily changes (and of her body being sexualized in her interactions with boys and men) was less that of being overwhelmed than adopting an imperative of drawing distinctions between those settings where she could experiment with her embodied social power and those settings where such strategies were less available to her.[6] Nevertheless, Carol's determination to avoid the tedium and 'immaturity' of school (see Jude and Gina's conversation in Chapter 5) involved dealings with adult authority. Carol's way of handling intermittent cross-checks and periodic 'raids' on her truancy (she sometimes got caught by various male teachers) was, in her words, to 'charm them' (see Wolpe 1989).

Whilst this took place 'behind school doors' (I did not witness the scenarios Carol described), I can only suggest it worked, since she never seemed to get into any substantial trouble, despite an attendance record which must have been unorthodox by anybody's reckoning (see the postscript however). Carol told tales of being 'captured' as a truant by both male and female teachers: 'Also C said she'd been caught "bunking" on Friday by Mr Allen [her form teacher]. He apparently covered up for her in respect of higher authorities.' When I asked her why he had been so benevolent, she responded, 'Cos, he likes me' (field notes 7:40).

In another context, Carol and her friend Liz had been sent to the year head for some infraction during a biology lesson. When confronted by the head of year, Liz was apparently insufficiently contrite, leaving him no option but to administer a detention as punishment, whereas Carol, judiciously penitent, left him free to just 'tell her off'.[7]

Her inability to manage her relations with female authority (including her female teachers and her own mother) with anything like the success of her dealings with men is instructive. Her experiences with both the female head of year and her mother read like the Hundred Years War:

> Carol reports that her mother keeps a very tight supervisory reign on her whereabouts and yet she also tells me that she is allowed out 4/5 days a week! She additionally says that she had escaped out of the house for a 2.30 a.m. rendezvous with Ivan [one of her boyfriends] near the river. She had apparently used the drainpipe to effect her freedom, like all good schoolgirl heroines! (field notes 7).[8]

Ann Whitehead found in her study of rural Herefordshire that running away represented the main female fantasy (Whitehead 1976). Carol had written the following note to her then best friend Liz:

> Dear Liz,
> I don't give a fuck about home, I'm leaving, don't forget when you're 16 you're leaving too. Are you coming?
> Love Carol.
> Sorry about the red ink. It's the only one I could find.

Home was as oppressive as school. School was not only 'boring', it got in the way of Carol making herself into a 'proper young woman' (see the discussion of schooling 'getting in the way' of friendship in Chapter 5).

Characteristically Carol (like Jude and her group) was highly selective about those aspects of schooling she appropriated. She avoided, if she could, those lessons she graded boring and only clocked into those where she was able to contact her friends without too much interference.[9] In entering the field and in entering into a research relationship with Carol I became a modest part of the solution to Carol's boredom. I turn next to consider the personal, ethical and micropolitical dimensions of our field relationship.

'Meal tickets': femininity, friendship and feminism

Given that I constituted part of Carol's 'entertainment', I was always conscious that she might have positioned me as gullible – an older 'other'. This would not be surprising given the unequal and invasive nature of the ethnographic research relation. Ethnographic relations require maintaining, not unlike business or political relationships where 'there is no such thing as a free lunch'. I wouldn't have blamed her for converting me into a form of sport (see the story Sandra told me of 'wally watching' in Chapter 3).

Carol was certainly aware of the advantages of becoming my informant. She enjoyed both her status as my confidante, and my status as her 'dependant'. There were after all some material advantages of the trade. In the course of the fieldwork I frequently subsidized her leisure at the Pond Cafe.[10] I felt inclined to claim this modest redistribution of resources as a field site expense.

Our unspoken contract recognized that if she was to become a subject of my ethnographic text, I was to become a useful subject within her life, in and around school. Whilst not claiming that this was an equivalence – we occupied and continued to occupy subordinate and dominant positions of power in relation to each other – we did nevertheless constitute each other also as sources of pleasurable company, even if I too was involved in what Linda Measor (1985:63) has called the contradictions between 'entering another person's world and their perspective but remaining alert to its configurations at the same time . . . in aiming for ultimate rapport and yet treating the person's account both critically and sociologically'. Carol's realistic estimation of my professional interest, as well as my personal concern about her, were constantly referenced by her during our fieldwork time together. (She wrote on the cover of her research diary 'Diary for Val PRIVATE! ha ha ha'). However the transaction was not all one way. She frequently requested and was given information that she had been denied access to in other areas of her life.[11] It is hardly surprising that Carol appeared to calculate the costs and the benefits of our transactions. She had after all learnt to bargain her time and labour at home and at school. She presented herself as calculating about almost every relationship she had.

The following section discusses her investment in testing her power on the heterosexual as opposed to the school (or ethnographic?) market. I will consider next how Carol took up the seductive pleasures of heterosexuality. These explorations involve her in cultural practices outside of the school context and outside of feminine forms of peer friendship. The cultural forms of 'flirting', 'fancying' and 'dating' provided her education in heterosexuality.

'Doing too much too young': negotiating heterosexuality as personal power

> Most significantly, she is forced to relinquish youth for the premature middle age induced by childbirth and housework. It's not so much that girls do too much too young: rather they have the opportunity of doing too little too late.
>
> (McRobbie 1980:49)

It is *because* Carol had worked out that embodied power *cannot* be permitted to a (working class) schoolgirl that she gave up on schooling and turned towards acquiring the 'really useful (heterosexual) knowledge' that would assist her in the process of becoming an adult feminine subject (adapted from Johnson 1979). Carol's fast-maturing body gave her access to an identity in heterosexual femininity but she also realized that her body required constant cultivation to secure sexual power. It wasn't enough simply to have the physical attributes; these needed displaying and maintaining in a particular way that coded her as 'sexy'. However becoming 'sexy' was no more straightforward out of school than it was within its walls. Nevertheless Carol struggled persistently to 'become a (heterosexual feminine) somebody' (Wexler 1992).

She strategized a great deal about getting money so that she could do the necessary work on her appearance. She knew that heterosexual appeal had to be worked for and that her desirable body required working upon to maximize her chances of attracting men: 'Carol says she is going to get £250 worth of clothes from her aunt who insists on C wearing stockings and appearing a "proper dressed-up young lady"' (field notes 8:5).

Being a 'proper dressed-up young lady' was the respectable form of heterosexuality within Carol's community. She had ferocious rows with her mother about 'suitable' appearances which in essence were arguments about Carol being thought 'improperly', that is, too sexily, dressed. On one occasion Carol's mother attempted to stop her from wearing a dress of her own choice to her sister's wedding. Carol described the outfit as 'mint green with a low cut back'. Her mother told Carol to sew it up. She then bought her another 'safer' dress which Carol contemptuously dismissed as 'like a romper suit' being all 'babylike and frilly'. Carol was adamant that she wouldn't wear the substitute. It was only her mother's ultimatum in the form of a threat to ban her from the wedding that led to Carol eventually relenting. She went in a new, less sexy, third choice

dress. A schoolgirl persona in a womanly body is, of course, a well established icon of masculine erotica.[12] The fascination older men showed
in Carol was mutual. As she put it, 'with some girls it's black boys, with
me it's older men' (field notes 7:7).

Conversely, Carol's contempt for her male peers was very vocal. Some
poor undersized 13-year-old commissioned to ask her out at the behest
of his first year mate had the difficult task of mediation. Carol, in a very
loud voice so that the errand boy and the assembled company could
hear, confirmed that she didn't usually go out with anyone under 16. To
paraphrase her meaning, she wanted to see the organ grinder and not
the monkey (scenario described from field notes 2:110).

Schoolboys were discounted because men were more 'desirable'; they
were seen as more prestigious – having cars, money and jobs. The 'polit-
ically incorrect' and dangerous sexual politics of Carol's adolescence were
played out as she attempted to handle the sexual attention she attracted
and encouraged through having a sexualized 'underage' body.

Gayle Rubin had asked that the women's movement construct what
she termed 'a political economy of the sex-gender system' (1975:204).
A description of the power relations which constituted Carol's heterosexual microeconomy represents one local response to that demand. The
next section discusses how the relations of class, age, sexuality and
gender were co-constructed in Carol's (problematic) performance of her
cultural power.

Experimenting with heterosexuality 1: 'acting hard and streetwise'

Carol survived as a truanting working-class girl with little or no money
of her own through being 'street wise'. She had a good local knowledge
and knew those places outside of school where she could hang out for
free or cheaply without fear of being detected, that is, the park grounds,
the cemetery shed, the Pond Café, the prom and rec, all conveniently
adjacent to school (for the necessity of registration) but all places where
no teacher was silly enough to look.

Carol had developed a comprehensive friendship network amongst
young men in these various locations to provide for her leisure needs.
The groundsman at the adjacent primary school used to give her cigarettes. A local road sweeper, Brian, was chatted up for similar reasons.
She had a friendship with four cemetery maintenance workers. Her regular haunt was the cemetery shed where the young cemetery workers
offered her a 'safe house'. It was a place from which she could do 'reccies'
(to see her school friends at breaks or home-time) and from which
she might even sometimes return to school for favoured lessons or

favoured teachers, especially if the tempo of home/school surveillance hotted up.

A tatty, semi-domesticated outbuilding in the nearby cemetery may not be everyone's idea of the perfect retreat, but to girls with no material base to call their own this was heaven. Carol found warmth, cigarettes and companionship. She learned their life stories (she retold these in elaborate detail in a tone of flirty sexual innuendo).[13] The illusion of safety was broken one time. The cemetery gang's supervisor tried to assault her when she was there on her own with him. She said that her 'men friends' had between them arranged to chaperone her on successive occasions. This appeared to have worked. This strategy allowed her to maintain connections with the one important source of practical as well as emotional and social satisfactions.[14]

If her 'men friends' played an important part in providing shelter and company, her boyfriends were seen as providing more substantial material benefits. According to my field observations Carol had the following boyfriends throughout the course of time I knew her: Brian, 22 years old (field notes 4:36); Ivan, 32 years old (field notes 4:36); and Adrian, age 20 (field notes 8:4). In effect, this fast turnover in men was central to Carol's construction of herself as desirable. These 'relationships' were extremely short-lived but they were always characterized by Carol as 'serious romance' but it was 'romance' as social subsidy (Hey 1983).

Carol's boyfriend talk always contained details of money: how much they earned and how much they had spent on her (Hey 1983). She told me about their cars and their clothes. She was a genius at extracting expensive gifts and clothes from them. Brian had apparently lent her some of his designer clothes and when the relationship ended, he demanded them back. Carol triumphed in her version of the encounter: 'If you can get the jumper off my back and the boots off my feet you can have them back!' (field notes 6:7).

Another gloss of her relationship suggested more traditional sexual politics. Brian was said to have informed Carol that 'I'm going out with you if me and Michelle don't work out'![15] Carol's public account of boyfriends as 'meal tickets' is indicative of her taking up 'hyper femininity' as a 'hard' stance. She specifically sought the power which comes from a disavowal of sentiment, reserving sentiment for her diaries. Her 'hardness' (she was always the *femme fatale* of each crisis encounter with men) involved her in discounting her investments in the more emotional 'feminine' subjective pleasures of being a girlfriend. Her stance mimics in broad terms hegemonic masculinity (Connell 1987).

In comparison with 'respectable' working class girls, Carol is highly active within the practices of heterosexuality.[16] Gabbie and Amelia's diaries were full of pining and hoping. Amelia, like a large number of girls in the study, experienced her sexual desires as fear (see Hey 1988). In contrast, working-class girls (like Carol) who defy the code of 'respectability' by actively pursuing a heterosexual identity have been constructed by teachers as potential sex workers (Griffin 1982). Not only are they therefore scrutinized as 'slags' (see Lees 1986) they are also pathologized as unfeeling and hence unfeminine: 'It's the coldness that worries me. There are two now that I deal with. They seem so cold they never seem to care. I would try to cut down on the numbers and encourage some feeling' (social worker talking about 'promiscuity' in Hudson 1984:47).

Within this discourse there is no scope to admit girls' investments in heterosexuality in terms of either pleasure or desire – such motivations are clearly impermissible (Hudson 1984). Paradoxically therefore those activities which girls themselves come to see as *confirming* their femininity are read as its denial. Christine Griffin has alluded to the way some teachers 'read' girls as 'hard'. At its core lies a powerful ideological resistance to the idea of femininity as emotional disconnectedness. The expressions 'cold' and 'hard' come to stand for how certain sexually active working-class girls are positioned and understood (see Hudson 1984).

Do girls also come to represent, as well as experience, their 'femininity' as unfeeling? Carol was certainly constructed through these same categories by her girlfriends and to some extent took them up.[17] She explicitly described 'acting slaggy and hard' as a 'pose' which she explained as 'being flirty' and 'hanging round boys you fancy' and 'smoking and drinking':

VH: What's in it [for you] being hard and tough?
Carol: It's good fun but it can give you a bad reputation.

Whilst Cyndi Lauper might incite all girls to have fun, working-class girls like Jude and Gina and Carol clearly find access to it fraught. We have already noted that the Crossfield girls 'give up' on the position of 'hard' and its associated forms of fun (see p. 74). Carol insisted upon a different tack because she wasn't so easily intimidated by the label 'bad image'. Conversely Carol impersonated a self as being in control of her image and her feelings – in this endeavour her vulnerability was powerfully displaced.[18]

Carol had ample reasons to distrust emotional investments in others. Her own mother had been married three times; as she pungently noted, defending herself from the charge of being illegitimate, 'I'm not a bastard, I've got three dads!' (field notes 4). Given her experience of the serial nature of her mother's marriages, Carol probably and realistically reasoned, that it may not pay to get too attached. When it was suggested that her biological father might be getting back with her own mother, she had responded with a comment about his money and of how she could get him to buy her anything.

Carol's public sexual self-confidence, her assertiveness, her 'hardness', thus represented her resistance to the social forms of control exerted within schooling, female friends and her family, but it might well also have been a fairly crude psychological mechanism for managing emotional vulnerability and perpetual disappointment (field notes 8:27). Maybe the cultural resources of 'hardness' propose also a feminine response to brutalization (Willis 1977).[19]

Experimenting with heterosexuality 2: the discourse of romance: 'soft centres'

Carol did however write another femininity. Both her personal diary (CPD) and her research diary (CRD) are steeped in conventions of girls' comic book romances (Christian-Smith 1993a, 1993b; Gilbert 1993). CRD is interspersed with anticipatory romantic narratives whilst CPD is more sexually explicit.

Despite these differences, Carol's main cultural solution to writing desire was implemented through the ideological category of romance; both narratives were organized through its structure (McRobbie 1978, 1982a; Modleski 1982). For working-class girls, romance *is* the only legitimate justification for hetero(sex). It was only in taking up desire through the code of romance that Carol could translate her transgressive social power into an acceptable cultural shape (Holland *et al.* 1990). Her diaries therefore offer an altogether more ambiguous and contradictory representation than the public performances of 'hardness' allowed.

Unlike her public assertions – that she was in charge of hiring and firing her boyfriends – her diaries located her and them in the discourse of romance. The main personal plot of CRD was sex and its production, distribution and consumption in the conventions of romantic love. She embellished the diary in the following way:

Sex is evil.
Evil is sin.
Sin is forgiven.
So sex is in.

The principal subtext was preoccupied by solving the cultural conundrums, 'what is being a proper young woman?' and 'how can you be "feminine" as a schoolgirl, if you aren't supposed to be sexual?' Carol takes up the quest by writing an aspirational fiction/fantasy of romance in which the strongest ideological currency is the exchange of sex for love. This is Carol's first entry in her CRD:

This morning my mum woke me up. She asked me to look after the baby while she went to work so I said 'Yes alright then.' Afternoon struck so I took the baby for a walk down the High Road. I was listening to my head phones when Peter passed me. I shouted back to him and he stopped and walked back a few paces then said 'Hi'.

'Hi'. I replied.

'What have you been doing with yourself?' said Peter.

'Not much haven't seen you lately and where's Fella?' [Peter's dog]

'Well I moved to Centre Green and in my flat you're not allowed puppies or a cat.'

Oh Fella was such a nice dog as well.

So he said all of a sudden 'When are we going to make love?' I was surprised so I said 'Don't know'.

'Meet me over Garden House by the cafe' Peter said.

'Ok' [I] said.

I went over there at 1.30 p.m. and waited. He didn't turn up so I started to walk home. As I had just come up the subway there Peter stood talking to his mate. So I stood there waiting finally he came up to me and said 'Sorry I didn't meet you but I went everywhere to find my trainers.'

'Yeh that's alright'

'Forgiven?'

'Of course Peter you know I have to forgive you don't you because you are sweet!'

'Walk me to the other end of the subway?'

'Yeah why not'.

I walked Peter up there then he kissed me goodbye.

I said to him 'Will you be down the Pond Cafe?' so he said 'Yeah I still hang around there a lot.'

So I said 'Bye Peter' and went.

Carol's style captures exactly the softer conventions of the genre of romance, most noticeably its characteristic obsession with the theme of the saturation of everyday life with sexuality. In this case, however, it is the same mundane reality (in the form of Peter's lost trainers) which actually rescues Carol from the erotic dilemma of managing her desire of him and of his for her.

The text is accomplished through the discursive erasure of reality by romance. The 'Peter Story' starts with her in the role as her mother's domestic – shopping and taking her baby sibling for a walk – but meeting Peter works to transform the drudgery of being her household's domestic through the 'glamour' of her chance encounter. Cinderella motifs circulate in popular consciousness because they connect to working-class girls' immersion in household labour. Carol's diary entries usually begin with jobs or tasks she has been set by others – her mother, her younger brothers, etc. – but then domestic skivvying invariably leads to erotic encounters with a variety of boyfriends. Walking her dog or walking the baby are particularly helpful narrative and social devices for meeting men.

I was frequently with Carol at the time of her Pond Café scenarios with Peter. On one occasion she was urging her then best friend Liz to convey a Christmas card to Peter, a service duly performed with much giggling. This eventually solicited a cool nod and circumspect 'Thanks, Carol' from the recipient. She explained to me that she had got to know him one day in the café through petting his dog. She had decided he was distinctly 'fanciable'. He didn't actually become one of her boy-friends (according to her conversations with me) but he did obviously enter her list of desirable men.

Whilst the above text converts the banality of domestic life into a 'brief encounter', tracing a journey from boring chores to high drama, her other diary (CPD) tells a story which moves in the opposite direc-tion. In short, it traces the reverse journey from romance to domesticity. This alternative text tracks a story of tenderly rendered 'dangerous liai-sons' – tender because they are stories of care and passion but dangerous because the passions they represent threaten their subject, Carol, with losing control over her body. The discourse of romance in which she places herself as both a desirable and desiring subject – 'turning men on', 'feeling horny' – gives way under her recognition that premedit-ated protected sex is neither consonant with the generic conventions of romance and is certainly not consonant with working-class mores about female sexuality, namely premeditation equals slag. Carol brings the text to a close with worries about the fear of being pregnant and ends the diary by planning the name of the desired/dreaded child (see Steedman 1982): 'If it's a boy it'll be called Adrian Lee after the daddy. Girl – Lily Audra after my mum'. Here we have how the aspirational themes of desire and power as a 'proper young woman' is literally as well as materi-ally grounded (as well as being ground down) by working-class girls' lack of sexual and social autonomy. The relations described in this text and between this text and other aspects of Carol's actual experiences are con-sidered in the final section of this Chapter.

'Poor cow': seductions and exclusions

The last time I met Carol at her behest, she was still living at home, manag-ing to evade school, cultivating sets of male friends, falling out with her female friends, involved in some showdowns with her mother and her mother's friend's children. She said that she was generally trying to 'make the best of a bad job'. She was talking enthusiastically about becoming a garage mechanic (she claimed her auntie and mother would provide

the financial support for the training). This ambition was typically contrary. She had not studied any relevant subjects at school. It was also a
surprising desire in someone who had put a great deal of her psychic
and social energy into becoming 'feminine'. She talked enthusiastically
about the anticipated pleasures of leaving home and having 'a flat of my
own' (note the similar dream held by Gina and Jude in Crossfield School,
discussed in Chapter 5). However, it is difficult to see how Carol could
translate her fragmented and incoherent plans into reality. She had no
qualifications. Social and economic dependency on boys and men was
not the passport out of the material situation of economic dependency
on her family.

The world of work and the sexual marketplace are sites in which
Carol was seriously interested but also seriously disadvantaged. It has
been shown in numerous theoretical and empirical accounts (and it has
been borne out in this research) that working-class girls are locked within
a culture which denies them rights to both bodily and economic autonomy (Holland *et al.* 1991; Holland 1993), a situation which has been
exacerbated by government legislation complicating teachers' respons-
ibilities to their pupils in terms of sex education rights and confusing girls
in terms of their rights to be treated and treated with confidence. As a
result the UK has one of the highest teenage pregnancy rates in Europe.

The sheer impossibility of Carol actually acting as a responsible subject
in ultimate and material control of her own body was borne out by a
subsequent letter, written to me by Melly, one of her friends after she
had left school:

> Well we've all left school now except Dottie who has gone back.
> But Liz, Amy, Carol, Rita and me have all left. Liz works at IBM
> doing office work. She likes a good drink she's always down the
> pub. She's got a new boyfriend called Simon he's a nice bloke I
> really get on with him. Amy, we don't see much of her 'cos she
> keeps herself to herself. She's also doing office work. God knows
> what Rita is doing? But Carol left school before she was meant to.
> I don't know if I'm allowed to say anything but she had a miscar-
> riage. She fell down some stairs. Her mum chucked her out so her
> brother's girl friend could move in. Poor cow eh?
>
> (letter from Melly, field notes 9)

It is hard not to concur with Melly, or hard to have contrived circumstances which could have prevented this particular outcome. What sort
of intervention would have been possible? How would it have been
possible to stop Carol from using the only form of power that she be-
lieved that she had? The appeal of 'a woman's right to choose' are a long
way from the material realities which construct forms of available sexual
transactions for working-class white girls. Here as we have seen, modes

of class sexual control work as sexual fear, or are resisted through ideo-logies of sexual 'excess' – 'turning them on' – so easily leading to 'getting carried away' and pregnancy.

Carol had not bought the ticket to self-improvement through merito-cratic escape – the glamour of work was of less immediate appeal than the glamour of being a woman and of pushing your own baby as opposed to your mother's. As a white working-class girl who positioned herself and who was positioned as marginal to the education system (see the girls in Mac an Ghaill 1988; Mirza 1992), she insisted on taking her chances in another desiring system. How else could she have been ad-dressed? What other forms of 'maturity' and femininity were available?

Yet she was not simply a sacrificial victim of the hopeless dream of desire proposed by heterosexuality. She was both seducer as well as being seduced by the promise that heterosexuality carries. An insistence on her rights to pleasure and amusement – her 'transgressions' or being 'naughty' to use Gotfrit's (1988) expression – represented however, only short term success in the face of the capacity of others to limit, exploit and appropriate her. Her insistence on pleasure was ultimately bought at the price of her own education. Lacking the cultural capital to become financially independent rendered her even more likely to invest in men as the only form of escape into 'the good life'. This is not an ideal posi-tioning from which to exercise autonomy and personal control.

Jane Miller (1990) speaks of the need to explore the ways in which hegemony is established through this terrain 'within an analysis of civil and potentially non-violent control'. She sees the metaphor of seduction speaking about 'the relation of women to predominantly male and het-erosexual cultures'. In so far as Carol's text is a text of seduction and in so far as the politics of heterosexual seduction present themselves in a more unmediated form outside of the relationships of girls to each other, Carol was the more easily seduced because she had left both schooling and her girlfriends behind.

This is neither a reprimand of Carol for showing 'false consciousness', nor is it a simple minded advocacy of female friendship (see earlier chap-ters) but it is to note the absence of a perceived viable alternative suf-ficiently seductive or attractive enough to make a difference to Carol and girls like her. The struggle to make a feminist politics of education has to attempt to construct *realistic* as well as *pleasurable* options for diverse girls. I am not under any illusions that we will find any simple answers to the complexities we live as subordinates within dominant relations.

The point of understanding Carol is to understand her as active within arenas of experience discussed neither in school nor at home. She was inventing by cultural means her own version of how to become the fascinating object of masculine desire. She strove to be, but could not become, the heroine of the romance of heterosexuality. Such places and destinies are for dreams, fantasies manufactured in Hollywood films or in Australian soaps. She was simply working with the raw materials of what cultural and social power and pleasures she both imagined as well as embodied, as she searched for 'proper young womanhood'. But she was also doing what we all do given that we are compelled to work within popular and dominant forms, namely that in so doing we allow our consent to our own regulation:

> We make sense of our experiences in ways that attempt to resolve the contradictions of the self that are created and lived within dominant forms. An individual's inscription into the culture becomes a process of negotiated consent, not coercion, marked by moments of refusal.
>
> (Gotfrit 1988:128)

Notes

1 When I first met Carol, Gill was the designated 'best' friend. In mid-September, it was Amy, and by the end of the same month, Maria. However, by the start of the next year, it had shifted again to Liz. Apart from the cigarette débâcle I never ascertained why someone was 'in' and someone 'out'.

2 This dilemma was particularly acute because the data derives from public and private sources. I have multiple 'Carols' to choose from. Which Carol am I to offer the reader? – the private Carol who gave me her unsolicited private diary at the beginning of my field work at Eastford (Carol's private diary, or CPD) or the Carol she wrote about in another diary in response to a research request (CRD), or her friends' Carol? Furthermore what degree of attention and emphasis should I place on the public persona, who was marginalized and self-marginalizing in school? How is it possible to represent her without voyeurism? In a sense this dilemma is intrinsic to all ethnographic data and its analysis and interpretation but it was my especially close relationship to Carol that made any representation of her 'multiple selves' extremely difficult. This was because so much of who she was resided in constantly shifting, contradictory versions through which Carol proposed her femininity as public performance as well as private investment.

   In editing the case study I have decided to focus upon data generated in or reported in real time field work situations. This has meant the practical elimination of her private diary (CPD), apart from a summary, on the grounds that the content was private material. This goes to the heart of the dilemma, however. Feminist and indeed all ethnography has as its conditions of production highly personalized field work relations – inside of which people are amazingly prepared to allow the researcher privileged access to their lives, though, as researchers note, the relatively powerless make 'easier' subjects (or, some would say, 'targets'; Stacey 1988). I have not resolved these issues in this text. See the discussion in Chapter 3.

3 It is inappropriate to go into too much detail here; the point Van Mannen

makes about 'vanity ethnography' or the 'confessional style' is well taken (Van Mannen 1988). But the resonances of Carol's strategies to my recollections of the 'bad girls' I envied and admired/feared at secondary school provided another way into understanding 'ethnographic' Carol. For example, one of my best friends at secondary school, once 'traded' with the manager of a shop a touch of her breasts for some cigarettes. I remember thinking at the time that having breasts must be wonderful because men were so evidently in their thrall. It was not so much that men were oppressing women, more that women and girls had things that men would die for.

4 This is true of all the girls, but it is the particular intensity of the fieldwork relationship with Carol that I am referencing here.

5 We were walking round the 'rec' (recreation ground), a grassy area near a large outdoor swimming pool, at the time.

6 I am *not* implying that school was sexually neutral (see Epstein 1995), merely that it was a question of degree, as my discussion of Carol's 'flirting' and 'charming' makes clear.

7 Later on in the conversation, when we were discussing this situation, Carol observed that 'Mr Clay [the year head] likes me, he gets on with me'. Despite the fragmentary nature of the evidence one way to construct Carol's success is to see her working her 'charm' upon some male teachers (see Wolpe 1989).

8 Carol's personal diary (CPD) was full of comments about illicit meetings and of her 'sneaking out' from under her mum's 'nagging'.

9 There is a literature on schooling and boredom. It is heavily gendered in the direction of exploring boys' boredom and their responses to it (see Willis 1977; Everhart 1983; Nelsen 1987).

10 As a persistent truant Carol couldn't take advantage of free school meals and trying to sell the meal ticket meant a risky entry into the school premises.

11 For example Carol asked about contraception and reproduction. The pertinence of these requests will be shown later (see Oakley 1981 for the impact of research upon the research subjects; Brannen *et al.* 1991).

12 The image can be traced in popular, élite and pornographic literary culture, both *The Belles of St Trinians* and Nabokov's *Lolita*. Evidently many men seem to find the juxtaposing of the 'innocent' powerlessness of the schoolgirl within the physically developed body of a woman erotically indispensable.

13 Carol represented her alliance with these men in jokey tones, suggesting that it was a 'safe' place.

14 Carol also expressed her sexual power in 'fancying' older men. The only older man I saw who she singularly failed to charm was the unsavoury proprietor of the Pond Cafe, who I suspected reserved his pleasure-seeking to seeing how many times he could recycle his chip fat!

15 This was how Michaela spoke about Carol splitting up with Brian.

16 I am using the indigenous term of 'respectable' to draw a (crude) distinction between those girls who indicated they were sexually active and those who indicated they were not.

17 Being called 'larrupy' is an important indicator here. More generally in patriarchal western societies feminine desire is widely pathologized and is always capable of being permeated and contaminated by social disapproval,

which then sediments as feelings of badness/sluttishness/slagginess. The pleasures of the flesh are endlessly paid by the guilt induced by the mind (see the discussion in Chapter 7).

18 Her diaries are full of terse details about being 'packed in' – '6th October he packed me in because I was talking to other people' – private comments which contradict her public pose (see Jude and Gina's description of heterosexual processes as about increasing degrees of masculine 'ownership').

19 Previous accounts have read 'hardness' as ideological, not as an actual material set of practices. I am not aware of any substantive work done on examining how girls can enjoy being 'hard' (see Jude and Gina's fleeting enjoyment; see also how Princess's 'hardness' was positioned as illegitimate).

Chapter 7

YOUNG, GIFTED AND WHITE: MIDDLE-CLASS FEMININITIES

Academic girls and the heterosexual economy of the sixth form

I first encountered one of the most prestigious groups at Eastford School in the fifth form. This group comprised a trio of highly academic upper middle-class girls: Suzy, Lara and Barbara. Their star status was confirmed when a teacher, assuming that this was the only group involved in the study, asked me why I had chosen to study this group rather than 'ordinary' girls. To illustrate their 'uniqueness' she told me the following story. It was a custom for staff to buy students who took part in school plays a soft drink at the end of the production run. Lara ordered a brandy and orange – a preference that sealed her reputation as the urbane 14-year-old she aspired to be. Sophistication was the élite's hallmark.

The 'all-stars' poise was predicated on affluence and expressed through classed patterns of leisure, aspiration and (in)conspicuous consumption. The threesome had substantial clothes allowances. They were good skiers. They were all fluent in at least one other language. Their academic and social accomplishments advertised substantial parental investment. Typically Barbara and Suzy had theatrical ambitions, and all three dominated school drama productions.[1] Suzy and Lara undoubtedly took up the role of star pupils, spending their lower sixth year preparing for Oxbridge entrance. Their teachers variously enthused over the trio's attitude and academic abilities.[2]

Little else in the course of my fieldwork went as smoothly as my fieldwork relationship with these girls.[3] They were very accommodating, our relationship in part established through our similar class position. By involving Suzy and Barbara (Barbie) in the research I had confirmed them in the belief that they were everything the school had said they were: bright, articulate and personable – ideal pupils, ideal girls and ideal research subjects.

In addition to their high status derived from being achieving girls, they also accumulated prestige from their respective places in a more volatile (heterosexual) economy of the sixth form. Their own network was combined with a wider well-established boys' network formed in the fifth year. This grouping currently comprised the trio as well as Paul, Duncan and John. These six co-jointly created what the girls had originally referred to as a 'platonic' bond.[4] Their platonic alliance provided additional support amongst others similarly defined as 'snobs', 'pseuds' or 'boffins'.[5] Suzy in particular was aware of her 'goody goody' image.[6]

However, the presumption that it was possible to conduct their peer interrelations with the élite boys in a sexually neutral way was becoming increasingly untenable. The girls described their former platonic friends as coming back from the summer term 'as if they were on heat'. Entry into the sixth form appeared to signal a rite of passage into an intensification of the (hetero)sexualization of relations. All three girls characteristically commented upon this change, though they repudiated the boys' aspirations by noting their 'poor taste'. Suzy remarked candidly, 'They wouldn't have a hope in hell if they didn't wear nice clothes'. If boys were to convert themselves from 'boy friends' into 'boyfriends' they would (according to the girls), have to raise their sartorial/aesthetic standards.[7]

The compulsion to sort out what it meant to be acceptably feminine was intense. It was driven by the demands of the boys and the competitive relations between 'different' girls as well as the emergence of desire. The main social dramas of the all-stars' sixth form life surfaced out of the pressure to become a boy's girlfriend as opposed to remaining a girl's girlfriend. The theme of transferring and negotiating shifting allegiance plots the main storyline of this Chapter.

If we recollect the trio's performance of 'taste' (Chapter 2) – Top Shop for the masses and Warehouse for themselves (the names of the respective shops actually contradict their status) – we can anticipate the second theme of this Chapter: distinction. In other words the ways in which the all-stars switched from homosociality to heterosexuality amplified the academic distinctions already put in place. As we will see, the élite participated in the practice of locating themselves academically through judging (and being judged) against 'other' (non-élite) girls. The use of working-class girls as a negative reference group also allowed the all-stars to measure their success as 'appropriately' feminine subjects (see Chapter 6).

However, whilst Barbara, Lara and Suzy co-jointly defined themselves against the 'proles', they did not share an identical position. Their divergent views on boys and the desirability of dating created significant tension, even though between Lara and Barbie there was a significant

convergence of practice. Only Suzy stood out against the pressure to conform. Their debates about their attitudes to the business of boyfriends
and dating organized the terms of their discussion with each other and
with me. This debate over heterosexuality was conducted at two levels:
inward narratives of difference lived as personal 'choice' but it also
involved marking out collective class and gender territories in opposition
to the 'other'. Whilst the former motif mapped the trio's different investments in heterosexuality, the latter charted the girls' shared privilege as
bourgeois subjects.

Middle-class girls' narratives of femininity: 'dykes', 'jailbait', 'filmed through Vaseline'

The social demands of becoming a girlfriend problematized the girls' taken
for granted primary commitments to each other (Griffin 1985; Griffiths
1995).[8] Suzy particularly regretted the loss of her place as Barbara's
'significant other'. She resented the privilege attached to what she termed
'the sacredness' of boyfriends. Barbara too reflected, 'That's the thing,
it's always different if there's a boy around'. Despite this shared recognition
Barbara and Lara enthusiastically transformed themselves into girlfriends
(during the course of the fieldwork Lara had a 'steady', Patrick, and Barbie
had several boyfriends). Only Suzy resolutely refused the role of girlfriend, although the pressures from Duncan and her friends to become
his girlfriend were substantial. These differences emerged around several
themes – ideas of themselves as desirable and 'attractive' (Hollway 1984)
and critical ideas about the social penalties of conforming to the conventions of 'dating'.

Barbara's position as a self-accepting 'desirable' girl was almost unique
amongst the girls I interviewed. Ironically only one other girl, Carol (the
girl most likely to have been evaluated through the élite girls' label of
'jailbait'), identified herself as 'attractive enough'.[9] Neither Suzy nor
Lara liked their 'looks'. Suzy described herself as 'wide'; Lara claimed
she was 'dumpy' but unlike Suzy, Lara heavily invested in an identity
as a girlfriend. She was frightened, she said, of 'being left on the shelf'![10]
As 'Claire', one of Wendy Hollway's (1984) interviewees says, 'There
is a hell of a lot of pain around not being attractive enough and particularly about not having boyfriends'. Suzy recalled feeling dissatisfied with
her body very early on in her childhood, citing a huge scene she had
with her mother at the age of 5 as evidence:

> I was supposed to go to school and I just sat in my room, everything
> I tried on I *hated* and I took it off and I had a *massive* scene with my
> mum and I shrieked and bawled and I told her how much I *hated*

my clothes . . . and there's always been a thing about going shopping with my mum to buy clothes and I've got memories of standing there in the changing room weeping 'cos I hated the way I looked.[11]

Walkerdine (1987) has argued that the 'mastery of reason' throws into question claims to feminine identification, but it is a split which Suzy paradoxically intensified by refusing the 'solution' of heterosexuality. Suzy enjoyed her 'cleverness' and argued that her refusal to have a boyfriend was a positive rather than a negative choice. She defended her 'celibacy' through the theme of individual rights (see Saskia, Chapter 4). Here Barbie and Suzy are debating about 'commitment'; Suzy comments:

There are all those pressures and everything and then I think to myself, 'Come on, you are still at school, you're only 15. It doesn't matter what you do' . . . I mean it does matter what you do in the eyes of others but when it comes down to it, it doesn't matter if I have 10 boyfriends or no boyfriends at all because *what I want for myself is what I should have.* And I have got what I want at the moment basically . . . I mean . . . sometimes I think I've said this millions of times before, at the moment, for what ever reason it is, 'Yep, I'm sacred of physicalness or whatever . . . scared of commitment or responsibility or whatever' . . . I mean it's probably all of those things.

Interestingly Barbie picks up on an apparent contradiction in Suzy's rationale, 'But you can't be scared of commitment, you're committed to me and Lara!' Suzy still insists however that 'commitment to a boy' is 'different'. She goes on to explain that she saw other girls with their boyfriends and that she didn't like what she saw. Her discourse draws upon themes of ownership and control (resonant throughout other data when girls talk of heterosexuality) in terms of girls being 'bound to men', of not being able to 'shake off' the attachment to boys. She summarizes her own feelings of resistance to 'romance' as 'just a sort of vague anxiety'. At the same time that Suzy is developing this theme of resistance, Barbie is contesting it and Suzy's position:

Suzy: I know I don't really want to go out with anyone. I've got a lot of other things to do in the meantime . . . [two seconds' pause]. That's really my mentality. I don't . . . I *can't* be *bothered*.

Barbie: But I'm always very wary when you say you *can't* be bothered. Is it because you can't be bothered or is it because you're scared . . . scared of what you're getting into and scared that you'll become like Lara and Patrick?

Here the reference is to Patrick's possessiveness. Suzy thinks of predict-abilities and 'habits' as wearisome but Barbie still interrogates what she sees as another agenda around 'fear':

Suzy: I really don't *want to*. I can't fit it into my life . . . for god's sake.
Barbie: Well you've just given up an A level so you could fit it into your life.

Barbara linked Suzy's refusal to her low self-esteem, 'because you don't like yourself enough'. Suzy did not dissent from this view, though she still claimed (somewhat equivocally it has to be said) 'and I have got what I want at the moment basically'.[12]

Unsurprisingly the intensities of their own relationship with each other and the intensities of the competing attractions of heterosexuality sur-faced early on as a major theme. Suzy's awareness that Barbara was keen to become a boy's girlfriend unbalanced a previously reciprocal relationship. They explored these tensions through reconstructing a key moment in the form of a retell about when these differences first ap-peared in public.

The power of retells in girls' cultures of friendship was constantly dis-played and these girls were no different. Placing an event was a way to rehearse the tensions in current relations and thus check out the status of the friendship (see Chapter 5). We have met the practice of retells before and it is important to note that such retells were not always de-livered as the result of a specific request for information. Revisiting events, especially the most troublesome ones, created a chance to deploy a range of cultural knowledge concerning the self and the other. Potential new meanings could be derived by revising interpretations or just as likely old conventions and certainties could be confirmed. In this episode the girls return to a current hot topic:

Suzy: No, I don't think you're thriving on . . . I mean dwelling on . . . thinking constantly 'I've got to get a boyfriend'. I know, come on, that you're not going to do that. 'Cos other things enter your mind, but obviously . . . but I . . . but at [the res-taurant] last week I just felt sort of . . . 'cos we had a conver-sation about 'em . . . how you wanted a boyfriend *desperately* and I said 'Yes, I know you do,' and then you got really angry with me for making you eat the hamburger [laughs].
Barbie: [Laughs]
Suzy: God! I felt like we were a married couple.
VH: [Laughs]
Suzy: . . . We were . . . I was paying for her, lending her the money to pay for the hamburger . . . and she left her hamburger.

Barbie: I thought you were more like my mother.

Suzy: I thought you were joking when you said 'Well I ain't eat-
ing it!'. I kept going on at you 'cos I thought she's joking.
I was trying to see your face and in the end she got really
annoyed and she said: *'Look I'm not having the hamburger!'*
[mimics angry voice]. Oops! You were so angry, that's the
angriest I've ever seen you. It was over such a poxy thing.

Barbie: No, but I'm getting really angrier over lots of things at the
moment . . . don't know why . . . It's nothing.

Suzy: And because we'd just had that discussion about you know,
you wanting a boyfriend, I was really quiet and my irrational subconscious or conscience [*sic*] or whatever started
racing away . . . 'Christ, you know, she doesn't want to be
here . . . she wants . . . she'd much rather be here with a boy
and all' . . .

Suzy's replayed episode in which the rejection of food is linked to the
girls' domestic drama about commitment is as sociologically interesting
as it is psychologically revealing. The identification of the offering of
food with nurturance and love has been the basis for work which tries
to understand how the psychic aspects of subjectivity are encoded in
highly charged cultural practices (Orbach 1986). Barbara's resistance to
Suzy's 'fussing' is definitive: *'I'm not having the hamburger!'* Suzy casts the
relational dynamics as those of 'a married couple':

Oh God, it was so horrible . . . Oh God [embarrassed] I really . . .
you've got no idea how much I felt like the wife and you were the
husband. I said: 'Eat your hamburger' [mimics nagging voice] and
you saying: 'I don't want my hamburger' [mimics child's].

What is striking is the girls' awareness of resonant voices from those
more public (and clichéd) forms within their own intimate private relationship. Suzy specifically claims the role of 'nagging wife', an interpretation explicitly rejected by Barbara, 'I didn't feel like . . . I did feel that you
were my mother, not my husband [she corrects herself] not my wife'.

Barbara positions herself instead as the victim of a 'bossy mother' (see
the discussion of the two Katies' note, pp. 34–5). The 'hamburger retell'
encodes aspects of the psychological and social drama of the girls' struggle, as Suzy's comments indicate. She is aware that beneath the trivial
social details was an underlying disturbing presence – the existence of
counter-attractions: 'Christ, you know, she doesn't want to be here . . .
she wants . . . she'd much rather be here with a boy and all. It's just
really weird'. This comment created a 10 second silence. The continuing distress caused by these 'irrational', 'subconscious' or 'conscience' (*sic*)
thoughts emerged powerfully as a major sequence in our 'discussions'.[13]

Suzy shifts the ground to take up the theme of rejection even more forcefully:

> I just feel like at lunch time and at break you're really more and more and more . . . you just sort of sit there really quiet and then when Lara and I say something to you to stop you from being quiet . . . you just snap at us . . . and at times like that I just start thinking . . . If she wants a boyfriend, right *let her fuck off and get a boyfriend and just leave me alone*, because . . .

Suzy is then lost for words: 'I get so sort of . . . just . . .' She cannot name this emotion. She is compelled to silence – split from the knowledge of what she feels because such feelings implicate her in the 'illegitimate' discourse of lesbianism. I move to acknowledge (legitimate) the impact of Barbara's boyfriend on Suzy:

VH: Did you feel upset by her decision to go out with David?

Suzy: Yes, I felt really upset and half of me felt, 'Right! This is it, you know, the end of the relationship, never see her again' [self-dramatizing tone].

Barbie: Really? [surprised]

Suzy: And the other half thought, 'For God's sake, this is only the beginning . . . you've known Barbara for almost two years, don't be so bloody stupid. It doesn't matter that she's got . . . and I really like David as a person [said in an adult/serious voice].

Barbara guiltily rehearses her position, 'I'd had all these discussions after Keith and Rod [two previous boyfriends], "I won't do this I won't say this".' However her 'lightning romance' with David ('I'd only known him a week') contradicted her intentions. No wonder Suzy retorts, 'I know, but I'm not your master. You can do what you like.' Suzy, however refutes her putative disinterested stance when questioned about the negative effect that David has had on their relationship:

Suzy: I think the thing that I found most horrible about it was that we never actually spoke about it. I think that we were too scared to actually say . . . I just wished you'd said to me something like . . . 'Are you upset?' . . . or something?

Barbie: [Interrupting, insistently] I did! I did! I did . . . I asked you thousands of times . . .

Suzy: [Interrupting] When?

Barbie: And you said 'No'.

Suzy: You didn't ask me thousands of times.

Barbie: I remember distinctly asking you one time at lunch time.

The disparity between the 'thousands' and the 'one' reveals the force of Suzy's claims on her – and Barbara's own reluctance to confront the delicate issues of negotiating 'ownership' in changed conditions. My presence enabled Suzy to confront Barbara with her anger about being ditched in favour of a boy:

> I also felt as if . . . I never really saw you at breaks or at lunch times because you were talking to David all the time and Lara sort of standing around talking [to her boyfriend Patrick] and then you were talking to him all the time, all the time, all the time and I said . . . 'Are we doing anything on Saturday night?' And you said, 'No, I'm going out with David' . . . Huh! No, it's just a bit of a shock apart from anything else [three seconds' pause] I think the whole thing has made me think that I should be a lot more independent . . . And sort of . . . yes it has . . .

Barbara acknowledges:

> You're bound to look at things differently, if someone else . . . I mean . . . it was as if we'd got rid of Jamie [a boy with whom the two of them had a semi-platonic, flirtatious relationship], and there was just us two, and I'd gone along and brought another boy into it.

Like other studies have shown, the girls do not simply 'deff each other out' (see Griffin 1985; Griffiths 1995). Even if Suzy represents the loss of Barbie in dramatic terms, their own talk also demonstrates that a great deal of emotional labour was expanded in trying to manage their relations around boys, even if they did not always succeed.

Nevertheless it is important to remind ourselves of the resistance Suzy has shown to heterosexuality and to boys taking over her friend. She has not been the fragile and 'sensible' rational middle-class girl. My claim is not that she was struggling to become a lesbian. It is rather more that these girls are caught without a language in which they can claim their interdependency through all its aspects – its irritations as well as its pleasures, its erotic as well as its social compulsions (Griffin 1995).

Above all else it was the systematic cultural presumption of hetero-sexuality which called into question the legitimacy of the girls' close relationship with each other. Both girls had already been given the label 'lesbians'. This emerged in the course of their reading and commenting upon my field notes:

Suzy: [Looking at my text] Why does it say here 'Zoe rumour'?
VH: Oh Zoe, the third year girl, do you remember she came across, we were all in the playground I think . . . near the wall . . . you know near the wall where you used to stand, near the wall with the marks.
Suzy: Yes.
VH: Jamie was there at the time, sort of hanging around and Zoe

came across and said something . . . 'Do you know there's a rumour going around the sixth form about you two . . . about lezzies or something . . . ?' And I don't know if Suzy or you Barbara said 'Oh it's all right, we've talked to somebody about it'. Do you remember the reference?

The girls puzzle over the identity of the girl who was spreading this specific rumour:

Barbie: I think I know who you mean [referring to Zoe] because there was a 'Liz rumour', because I thought you'd got mixed up with Liz.
VH: *Another* rumour!
Barbie: 'Cos you know . . . told you . . . remember I was telling you Liz had come up to us in the corridor once when I first went around with those two [Suzy and Lara] and [she] said 'Do you know that people in the sixth form think you're dykes!'

These incidents confirm the ubiquity of the term as a controlling mechanism (see earlier Chapter 2, Chapter 5). The girls' response is to take the matter home:

Suzy: I remember not one of us knew what a dyke was.
VH: [Loud giggles] So you wouldn't realize it was an 'insult' anyway?
Suzy: 'Some people think you lot are dykes' . . . I remember we went . . . 'Oh! Oh! Do they?'
[All of us giggle]
Barbie: So I went home and I said to my mum, 'What's a dyke, mum?'
Suzy: *Did you?*
VH: What did your mum say?
Barbie: My mum said they are sort of butch [or] lesbians.
VH: What did your mother say, Suzy?
Suzy: She just said 'lesbian'.

As Sue Lees (1986:72) remarks in another context:

A reputation cannot be clearly and unambiguously redeemed even by physical victory in the same way as it can either by a boy proving his 'bravery' or for that matter, a clear competition between girls for boyfriends. But, ultimately the very vacuity and ambiguity of the term 'slag' is, as I have argued, a reflection of its role in the control, by males of girls' freedom.

The term 'lesbian' works in a similar way, but as I argue elsewhere in the book, its deployment (like the term 'slag') is not confined to boys.

On the contrary it takes a particular force *because* it is applied by girls to each other. More specifically the power of the word 'lesbian' to control girls is secured precisely because girls *do* experience their relations with each other as a passion.[14]

At one point in our discussion Barbara makes the connection between the above episode and another instance where the term lesbian was again significant:

Barbie: That's another thing . . . I've just realized my mum says to me, '*Don't* wear that because you look, you look really butch'.

Suzy: [Shocked] Really!

VH: Does she?

Barbie: Yes . . . and she says.

Suzy: Like what?

Barbie: Like . . . like . . .

Suzy: I like your suit.

Barbie: My suit, I know . . . I've never actually worn it out yet because . . . But it's . . . I really like it, it's all pin stripe grey and I was wearing a white shirt and she said, 'You shouldn't wear it'. I was wearing flat shoes and she said, 'You shouldn't wear flat shoes with that suit because you look . . . you look butch and people will think you're butch. You should wear shoes with heels otherwise . . .'

Suzy: Did she?

VH: Did she?

Barbie: No, no I didn't wear it because I haven't worn it yet . . . a friend of my mum's gave it to me.

Suzy: I think a suit looks horrible with high heels.

Barbie: Yes . . .

Suzy: I think it looks very tacky. You've never told me that before.

The double bind Barbara finds herself in is as ironic as it is instructive. In rejecting high heels as 'tacky', she is seen by her mother to be rejecting heterosexuality itself.[15] The impossibility of being 'right' replicates other evidence about girls' positioning in other discourses. Hudson (1984: 31), writing about girls and adolescence, quotes a girl who says 'Whatever we do it's always wrong' (see McRobbie 1980).

It is known that some girls resist the institutional attempt to eradicate opportunities for sexual self-display (Walkerdine 1986; Evans 1991). However we know far less about how families 'make people' through definitions of appropriate femininity (Holland 1995). Barbara's story is a fascinating example of this process in play (see also Carol's dress story in Chapter 6). It is a particularly powerful one because the intervention appears to have undermined Barbara's self-confidence in the fashionable feminine identification she has spent such a lot of energy cultivating:

VH: What's your reaction to that?

Barbie: It upsets and scares me because I like how it [the suit] looks, but I'm scared that people *will* think I'm butch, but then I get angry – does it really matter?

Suzy supports her: 'Why, it doesn't matter at all.' However, Barbara is unconvinced: 'But it *does* matter'. Despite trying to resist her mother's advice, Barbara still ends up in the position of thinking twice and, regardless of Suzy telling her, 'You looked really nice in it', she lets the subject drop. Letting subjects drop occurs when girls can see no immediate prospect of resolving their dilemma. Like silences and long pauses, it is an eloquent testimony to noisy 'differences'.

Barbara's difficulties are posed by her mother as those arising from a sexual misreading, whilst Suzy constructs the issue as about taste and individual rights of self-definition. The girls do not at this point propose that the fault lines of cultural contradiction run through femininity and its representation(s).

The only discourse that recognizes the political and performative nature of femininity is feminism and the only girl who made any serious attempt to resist the compulsions to 'normality' through the use of feminist arguments was Suzy. Given the contradictions of the girls' lives (between their class positioning in school as 'successful' and their gendered vulnerability in heterosexuality), we should not expect a coherent or 'pure' non-contradictory feminist positioning. We find instead the production of competing meanings – feminist moments amidst the making of bourgeois hegemony, acclamations of personal 'rights' – as well as a fleeting recognition that rights are unevenly distributed.[16] The following episode displays how these wider tensions are played out in girls' construction of meanings about femininity in the 'filmed through Vaseline' dialogue.

The girls had been reviewing an earlier transcript when we had also been discussing clothes:[17]

Suzy: It's really funny this bit [looking at the transcript]. You say, 'I feel feminine if I wear skirts, but you don't feel feminine if you wear trousers'. And I say 'But how, you're a female'. Then you say, 'When I say feminine, my interpretation of feminine is other people being attracted to me by being feminine', but I say 'You're attractive anyway and people are attracted to you all the time.'

Barbie: And then you . . . say 'Feminine as, erm, knowing that you are a woman and making sure that everyone else knows'.

Suzy: But why is it . . . why is it . . . why are women (this is the thing about the article again) supposed to make themselves look attractive for other people . . . I think a lot of women want to, but the reason they want to is because the whole society is conditioned so that women [are] filmed through Vaseline.

To Barbara, 'looking good' is simply the desire to 'please yourself' but Suzy argues that for a woman 'pleasing yourself' is always experienced as 'pleasing others'. Barbara senses the dangerous implications of her investment in the practice of 'dressing up': 'You can't just make a sweeping statement that it is just for blokes, 'cos I don't think it's true.'

Whilst Suzy's puritanical feminist position provides support for her own resistance to dating, it also and somewhat more problematically challenges the investment Barbara has in making herself attractive. Barbara had found a powerful form of pleasurable self-esteem, positioned as a desirable girl of the 'being attractive enough' discourse. It is precisely these cultural practices of heterosexuality that have been seen by some feminists as the worm at the heart of feminine resistance (Rich 1980; Leeds Revolutionary Feminists 1981).

Suzy's shift into a puritan counter-stance of feminist political correctness unavoidably inflects Barbara's motives for presenting herself as 'attractive'. In making herself suitably sexy, is she not also being a victim of male consumption? Might she also be colluding with the temptations of the flesh – a position dangerously akin to 'slaggy'? Numerous researchers have pointed out how adolescent girls' coercion into signing a 'contract with heterosexuality' incites and subsequently pathologizes their investments in producing themselves as its objects (see Bush and Simmons 1987; Rossiter 1994). Suzy and Barbie are aware how easily feeling feminine can imperceptibly slide over into feelings of 'slagginess':

Barbie: Whenever I want to feel . . . Because I wear trousers so much I get . . . I start to feel sort of tomboyish and 'cos if you wear trousers, I wear flat shoes, so I walk in a certain way [mimes clomp, clomp] and then what happens, I completely hate all my trousers and I've only got one skirt that I like . . .

Suzy: Every now and then *you get amazingly feminine* . . . white stockings . . .

Barbie: Yeh! White stockings, high heel shoes and a skirt and I feel really brilliant but just for one night, 'cos then *I think I feel such a slag* so then I go back to all my trousers . . .

VH: What is in the word slag for you?

Barbie: [Five seconds' pause] Well, it used to be . . . slag used to be people who wore tons of makeup, lacy tights and tight skirts but I wear lacy tights and I'm not a slag, erm . . . I always think a slag is someone who doesn't speak very well, a really horrible voice. Like a fisherwoman . . . who's just out to . . . erm . . . jailbait.

Suzy: I think of a slag as someone who's . . . just . . . there's lot of them around this school. They walk around sort of clicking their heels, sort of their bums swaying from side to side and they're caked in makeup. And it's so obvious that they are out to 'get the boys' really. That's it! That's what I'd say a slag is.

Even though Barbara recognizes intellectually that the definition is internally inconsistent – 'I wear lacy tights and I'm not a slag' – she still experiences herself as one – 'I feel such a slag'. This only intensifies the need she has to construct the category 'fisherwoman'.[18] Both girls have a powerful co-investment in projecting excessive (slaggy) sexuality onto working-class girls. On the one hand it allows Suzy to hold on to her feminist position by modulating its threat to Barbie, that is, Barbie is not a slag despite being 'amazingly feminine' (hyper femininity for the middle-class?) because real slags are constructed by their projecting excessive (slaggy) sexuality onto working-class girls. It is apparent that even Barbara's copious self-confidence is in danger of imploding under the weight of the complex cultural associations of active feminine forms of desire with a pathology. Indeed it is precisely because Barbara 'feels' her 'femininity' as a form of 'tartiness' that Suzy's feminist critique momentarily hits a nerve. It is of course ironic that the coalition of a particular form of feminist appropriation with a particular type of class inflection produces an intensification of 'othering' as opposed to its critique.

'Slagging each other off': social and sexual competition

However, at the same time that the élite girls constructed distinction between themselves and the working-class girls, the non-elite 'fishwives' confirmed the trio's minority place as 'marginalized others' of the wider school community. The all-stars were well aware of their 'envied and desired' position:

VH: Do you remember the time you got criticized for the way you dressed? I don't know if it still happens now so much 'cos you're in the sixth form and a lot of people seem to dress very similarly . . . erm, you were called 'tramps' . . .
Barbie: Hippies.
VH: Hippies . . . and other critiques and you said very powerfully on tape I remember, *'It's as if they hate us. They really hate us'.* What do you think they hated about the way you dressed? What was that about?
Barbie: We didn't conform.[19]

Suzy elaborates:

> They didn't understand it, I don't think. They thought it's some-
> thing different and you don't understand and if it's in the minority
> I suppose, then you sort of . . . to be immediately against it. I sup-
> pose . . . I don't know . . . Maybe also people really didn't like our
> image. 'We're the middle-class rich kids. We've got brains. We've
> got money. We've got weird clothes', you know we're . . . I think it
> puts a lot of people off. It did. It annoyed . . . everybody!

Here Suzy becomes her own semiotician, decoding how 'they' located
her image in the classic terms of a subcultural commentary. She understands the trio's 'trendiness' as provocative. The conceptual language of
class was a structured absence from the lives of working-class girls.[20] The
nearest they came to class discourse was in the submerged forms: 'snobs',
'boffins' and 'swots' (see McRobbie 1978; Frazer 1988). The all-stars conversely produced themselves through professing classed taste and classed
understandings. We have, for example, already noted how the trio constructed themselves as the apogee of modern bourgeois consumerism.
(see pp. 32–3, also Richards forthcoming).

By *being* the élite and dressing the part and by making their distinction
into a form of superior taste, the trio are staking claims as particular
beings on the public stage. Clothes purchased with one's clothes allow-
ance were supposed to signify appropriate class and sexual meanings. It
is not only Freud, however, who seems to have realized that stilettos
have a dense semiotic life; sexual and social meanings are multiple and
cannot be guaranteed, as the struggle about suits and high heels or lacy
tights and tight skirts discloses.

Nevertheless girls come to experience themselves as feminine through
their attempts to fix themselves and others through classed and hetero-
(sexualized) cultural practices. But they do not do so in conditions of
their own choosing; they can only do so through the prevailing relations
of power. Only by defining themselves against an *other* can claims *not* to
be snobs, boffins, slags, jailbait, hard or dykes appear convincing. By en-
unciating their femininity through the cultural articulations of class, girls
come to perpetuate their general subordination to hegemonic masculinity.

More specifically, because there are very powerful associations around
the meaning of cleverness as asexuality (Willis 1977) and as unfeminine (Walkerdine 1987), middle-class girls in Suzy's clique (apart from
her) were anxious to experiment with heterosexuality, often under circumstances almost as disadvantageous as those that working-class girls
encountered. Material wealth did *not* prevent Barbara from being subordinated through pejorative rumours spread by her male friends. Barbara's
position as the most heterosexually active girl in her group renders her
most vulnerable to the discourse of 'slag' and most conscious of the place

of appearance. Clothes and image are indeed 'loaded surfaces', but not quite in the way Hebdige (1979) and other subcultural commentators understand, because the loaded surfaces resonate with subjectively appropriated heterosexualized narratives about class and gender.

The co-construction of class and gender relations by both working-class and middle-class girls seals them into a mutual and apparently 'natural' antagonism (McRobbie 1978; Llewellyn 1980). However, there is another distant voice which can identify the pressures induced through having 'to be filmed through Vaseline' (Suzy). But it is a fractured voice (like working-class girls' common sense) and it is all too frequently silenced and self-contradicting.

The emergence of the feminist voice derived from my relationship with Suzy, as well as from her access to feminist literature at home.[21] However the appearance of Suzy's (puritanical) appropriation of feminism did not allow the resolution of her relation to Barbie, neither did it provide resources to enable them to think through Barbie's powerful attraction to heterosexuality's cultural forms. Her feminist views did not fully recognize either the pleasures of dressing up, or of being constructed as a powerful and desirable girl. On the contrary, the shift into critique raised as many questions as it answered and complicated rather than ameliorated the difficult issue of their different involvements in hegemony's competing seductions.

Moreover, as we have seen, the girls were incapable of sustaining a consistent counter-hegemonic position against hegemonic masculinity. On the contrary, they were invested in describing 'other' girls through its terms. Like Jude and her friends, Barbara, Suzy and Lara tried to inoculate themselves against the virus of inappropriate femininity, but since it was the discursive construction of femininities themselves which were to blame their quest was doomed.[22] After all, Suzy's resistance to losing her friend to heterosexuality and herself to 'boys' went hand in hand with, and was in fact overdetermined by, her stronger investment in a class position which slagged off her enemies – these were not, it has to be said, bourgeois boys but working-class girls. Becoming a girlfriend or resisting becoming one were simply variants on the theme of class – coded as a form of femininity or as a bourgeois form of feminism. Neither investments in the cultural strategy of middle-class trendy nonconformity, nor the cultural critique of 'semi-feminism', broke the powerful hegemonic claims of class and heterosexuality.

Notes

1 They were always given the leading roles. In fact Lara and her brother constituted something of a dramatic dynasty in school productions. I suppose it helped that their father and mother sponsored and ran the drama club.

2 Suzy was considered both beautiful and brainy. Lara was viewed as a very good 'all rounder' whilst Barbara was said to be the most 'stylish' though academically the 'weakest'.

3 Lest this appears complacent, Lara actually withdrew from the interviews.

4 Sexuality was, after all, supposed to be defined *out* of the places they occupied at the centre of the school (Walkerdine 1990; Epstein 1995). More confusingly still, school and familial ideology suggested to them that they construct their male peers as equals. That élite girls were socialized to consider themselves 'as good as the boys' was less the outcome of feminist beliefs (though these girls did have access to feminist and proto-feminist views about 'entitlement'), than of their parents' and their own investments in the academic values of the school.

5 Despite having the highest status in a meritocratic economy which valued brains, aptitude, good attitude and application, the élite occupied a less exalted place within the wider informal culture of the school. Here their 'hippie' style attracted a great deal of social antagonism (see later).

6 Suzy once told me of a time when her 'cleverness' and 'age' were used against her. Intriguingly she recalled: 'I think there was a girl who I was very good friends with at one point and then she turned on me, she still does it in a way. She always just likes to have one friend and when I tried to have other friends she wouldn't take it and she started to give me *absolute hell* for being 10 . . . and for being clever at the same time and I remember . . . this is the only time I've ever really regretted it.'

7 The trio were quite critical of the boys. They were also said to be 'immature'; one of the boys had also conceded the girls' superior sophistication.

8 Lara was the first of the trio to have a boyfriend. The girls described their friendship alliance as, 'Lara is still at the centre of it. Now she's going out with someone. Now our lives are sort of revolving around what she wants to do, but she still is the middle with us as the two side steps.'

9 'Jailbait' refers to middle-class girls' views that certain working-class girls' clothes and makeup conventions were 'too' sexual. I discuss the application of this term later in the Chapter.

10 Lara's relationship with Patrick drew heavy criticism from her friends on the basis of its exclusivity and its social and emotional demands. At one time Suzy had called Lara, Patrick's social worker.

11 At another time Suzy said that she was a 'a huge tank'. In fact, and predictably, these descriptions are contradicted by empirical reality. Barbie and Suzy shared each others' clothes. A lot of the girls' talk featured concerns over food, especially in the context of the pressures they were under at exam time. During one discussion Suzy said that she 'verged on anorexia . . . I remember when the exams were on . . . I used to make myself sick. I might as well admit it'.

12 There were extensive discussions amongst us about the history of the girls' platonic relations with their mutual male friends. Suzy felt herself under enormous pressure to become Duncan's girlfriend, but insisted that this would 'spoil' not only her relationship with Barbara but 'mess up' her friendship with Duncan. Space prevents me from fuller explorations about the élite girls' complex understandings about heterosexuality (see Hey 1988).

13 It is important to recognize the effects of research as a social process in all my research exchanges with the interviewees, in particular the ways in which these two particular girls positioned me in the exchanges. They frequently used my interest in understanding their friendship as an opportunity to speak to each other about difficulties which were previously unvoiced. Thus the girls would revisit past events through my presence as a way to mediate them.

14 It was evident that most girls were involved in intimate practices 'normally' associated with the privileged discourse of heterosexuality. They displayed open affection; kissed each other; held hands; walked arm in arm; made rendezvous; sent notes; and exchanged both gifts and confidences.

15 The word 'tacky' was part of the trio's lexicon about taste and it related to how the girls positioned working-class girls' style as 'tarty'. Both words carried meanings about 'cheapness', mass production and indeed of the masses themselves (see Chapter 2).

   Barbara's mother played a powerful role in defining her image. Barbara had mentioned previously that her mother would always intervene if she didn't like what Barbara was wearing.

16 In their different ways Llewellyn (1980), Skeggs (1994) and Frazer and Cameron (1989) all display similar evidence of girls' fragmentary, conditional and contradictory relations.

17 The girls enjoyed reviewing transcripts, remarking that it was 'like a video of our lives'.

18 The association between the working-class and sexual abandon is a historic discourse of Victorian 'reformers'. Evidence of its continuation is confirmed in moral panics about proletarian and black girls' sexual and social 'fecklessness'.

19 This comment is nothing if not ironic!

20 Such awareness is remarkably absent from the discourse of the working-class girls. The only other time it surfaced (obliquely) was when Sonia and Iris referred to Erin's clique as 'not their type of girl': 'Because they got their own money and they like going outside and going over to the bars and they haven't got a [free dinner] ticket'. Social power has a definite social and material space. Here is evidence that these two working-class girls have literally and metaphorically learned theirs.

21 I think the feminist voice owed a lot to the nature of our conversations about heterosexuality and feminine bonding and their coincidence with Suzy's own critical views about conformity (see Hey 1988).

22 Judith Williamson argues in the context of a critique of Cindy Sherman's parodied film stills that they ask us to: 'recognize a visual style (often you could name the director) simultaneously with a type of femininity. The two cannot be pulled apart. The image suggests that there is a particular kind of femininity in the *woman* we see, whereas in fact the femininity is in the image itself, it *is* the image' (Williamson 1986:92).

Chapter 8

GIRLS' CULTURAL AND SOCIAL IDENTITIES AND THE CONSTRUCTION OF HEGEMONY

'Women have always been divided against each other'.
'Women have always been in secret collusion'.
Both of these axioms are true.

(Rich 1979)

Introduction: s/educ(a)tions and social identities

The scene is the school playing field at Eastford. The fourth year girls are being organized for a session of track and field events. The girls begin their relay race. During the staging of the race the male head of boys' PE strolls onto the track accompanied by his class of boys. The girls' race is sabotaged. The girls merely begin again after the boys have gone. Neither their teacher nor they complain about one more random instance of their being rendered invisible.

What is going on? Either the boys were so self-obsessed as to be utterly oblivious to the events before their eyes or they were simply behaving to girls as masters to the servant class (Cock 1980). Social inferiors have neither to be seen nor heard and certainly do not have to be negotiated with. Girls conversely are generally denied the luxury of either being oblivious or of putting others into oblivion. The feminine is always on show and girls as a group have a particularly strong investment in understanding how social organizations function since they are usually placed in the most disadvantaged places within them (Arnot 1982).

One can surmise that managing their own oblivion by constructing feminine survival codes through forms of intimacy makes good practical and political sense. As we have noted, reappropriating the private creates opportunities for comment, critique and subversions of the masculine 'other' as well as the pursuit of their own important self-interests. Being thought not to be there does therefore have its delicious compensations not unlike those identified by Sartre when he describes how dominant language forms are nevertheless occupied and reworked by the 'dispossessed' who cannot be prevented from 'writing on the walls of his [*sic*] cell, from exchanging signs behind the guards' backs, with the other prisoners' (Sartre 1963:278).

Girls' occupation and defence of the realm of privacy is not unproblematic. Writing about their 'jailers' is one thing but writing about other girls another. When Erin and Saskia trade in the currency of inclusions and exclusions, when Jude and her clique seek to distance their current selves from their past alliances with non-Anglo girls, and when Barbie and Suzy mark 'distinction' upon their representations of the 'other' do we not also need forms of political address that seek to recognize the powerful poisons of intimacy, what Emmerson (1993) calls 'gynabuse'? Do not girls engage in forms of social harassment almost as damaging, and I would argue, at times even more damaging than those they experience through the discourses of boys, young men and older males? Aren't aspects of girls' cultures rife with the excesses of difference as power? Aren't girls' notes, for example, sometimes poison pen letters? Aren't we pretending that sexist oppression obliterates the myriad dimensions of other sources of power through which girls come to make themselves in conditions not of their own choosing but which they also can choose to mobilize? I have argued that it is not accidental that girls have a particular expertise in manipulating the local private economies of prestige because most of them are generally exquisitely attuned to how they function.

Equally we may cheer when the lone heroine resists the relentless conformity to become a (heterosexual) somebody. When Suzy says no, however tentatively or momentarily she does so despite the 'desertion' of her best friends, when Nina and Sally exchange condolences about the perfidy of boyfriends, we can also glimpse their shared insider knowledge. When Sally and Jude 'go crazy' in their 'transgressive' note, we laugh with them at the ludicrousness of the language of bombast and counter-claim. These and other instances signal a level of collective energy which persists in defining selves through words – to make their needs matter. Holding onto diaries and notes for years shows their importance (as sources of defiance as well as self-definition) and may also suggest the significance of acknowledging formative moments when the making of themselves was possibly at its most contested and all consuming. More nostalgically and bleakly it may also signify a loss of that flux and struggle as girls look back upon their younger more rebellious selves.

Whatever else is going on, girls are involved in substantially more than mere sociality when they construct 'the company they keep'. My interpretation has centrally addressed the power of hegemonic forms to recruit girls' social and subjective investments by the medium of friendship. It recognizes first, the regulatory bourgeois form of (compulsory) schooling and the supervening multiple divisions of power which the form encodes; second, the cultural imperative of heterosexuality – a form constantly incited but perpetually displaced within schooling; and third, how these cultural forces are played out either as the normalizing logics or anarchic illogics of practices which make up girls' compulsory homosociality. This chapter attempts the theoretical articulation of four major themes traced by each case study:

- the nature of the relations between the public and the private in schooling;
- the importance of subjectivity;
- the place of desire in girls' relations;
- the significance of divisions and 'difference' amongst girls.

The aim is to engender the generative but problematic concept of hegemony. The study has shown girls struggling to become, as well as defying the impulsions of becoming, 'normal' girls. It has found them intent on being social as well as sexual beings, critical as well as compliant subjects in their various positions as 'typical girls' or 'all-stars' – 'boffins' or as 'one of the girls'. The data has thus shown that the personal is indeed political, even if previously we have not thought to theorize girls' ordinary pleasures in each other's company as a source of meaning, let alone as forms of power and as sites of subjectifications.

'Living on the dark side': intersections between the public and the private in girls' cultures of friendship

Accounts of girls as marginal in youth subculture merely describes rather than explains the phenomenon. What we need is a recognition of the interrelatedness of male and female youth culture (Cockburn 1987). My reading of girls' same-sex relations establishes the vibrant (if subordinated) cultures of girls' homosociality as the material and ideological reality which lies on the 'dark side of a gendered youth culture' (Cockburn 1987:44; see also Griffiths 1995).

This sociology of girls' friendship has opened up narratives of 'lives lived out on the borderlands for which the central interpretive devices of our culture will not do' (Steedman 1986:5). 'Borderlands' are the empirical, as well as the conceptual space, to engender the model of school cultures, of girls as school subjects and of the ensuing relations of hegemony and counter-hegemony produced there.

This ethnography has after all emerged from out of the borderland/ marginal cultures of girls' friendship since these are one of the informal social contexts in which the girls are immersed.[1] Moreover it was only through insisting upon the significance of the minutiae of the everyday ordinariness of girls' friendship lives in the 'borderlands' at school – of practices dismissed as 'garbage' or 'trivial'; of feelings eliminated as 'immature'; of concerns pathologized as 'bitching' – that it became possible to recover aspects of the complex cultural codes within which different girls lived their personal relations with and against each other.[2] Girls' interpersonal affinities are, in other words, an ineluctable aspect of 'civil society', and are part of the network through which the forces of hegemony are variously installed (or contested) in culture.

Subject girls

Many feminist commentators have focused upon how schools construct their dominant gender code (Arnot 1982; Riddell 1989). My emphasis has been different. This study has discovered how girls take up school and community codes through their friendships. In understanding how girls performed their 'identity work' as friends, I have drawn upon the concept of subjectivity derived from poststructuralist analysis. Teresa de Lauretis (1984:182) conceives a materialist notion of subjectivity as 'a complex of habits resulting from the semiotic interaction of "outer world" and "inner world", the continuous engagement of a self or subject in social reality'. Alcoff (1988) and Lauretis (1984) both argue that the most generative location of a feminist theory of subjectivity is not in the notion of female self-essence, nor on the margins of the male tradition but in a self-reflexive analysis of the internalization of an engendered self.

How (girl) subjects live schooling subjectively (Corrigan 1987; Walkerdine 1987; Jones 1993) has been traced through an exploration of how girls' allegedly inconsequential friendship practices coded and were entangled within the densities and intensities of social division. This ethnography has explored how girls' groups reconfigured 'outside' class and gendered discourses as the 'inside' of their subjective and intersubjective relations. The cultural relations of girl friendship has also provided some oblique counter-discourses – moments of 'chaos/freedom' (Scheurich 1995) – instances when girls obliterated the invitation of hegemony. Yet the analysis has finally refused the simplicities of lionizing resistance (Steedman 1986), preferring instead to see the contradictions of girls' lives as cultural tensions lived in their friendship as lines of antagonism and solidarity – connection and disconnection.

Marginalia: 'the wild zone of women's culture?'[3]

Work by Jane Kenway and Jill Blackmore and others has identified the dominant place in schooling as white, middle-class and Anglo (Kenway and Blackmore 1995; see also Jones 1988, 1993; Mac an Ghaill 1994). Girls (and boys) who either do not carry these forms of identity/cultural capital (that is, they cannot be white, middle-class and Anglo) are nevertheless made subject to what Corrigan understands as the privileging of preferred forms: 'identities are (re)formed through the subjective objectification of this normalisation as a desire to be in "those places" so designated so approved' (Corrigan 1987:39: note 39).[4]

The invested desire to be approved retains its power even if the subject is aware that she cannot hope to make the criteria. But there are more 'places to be desired' than those guaranteed by the 'centre'. For example, Rutherford (1990:22) argues, that the centrifugal pull of dominant meanings in their turn provokes the creation of other cultural configurations capable of generating alternative, subversive and contesting desires and discourses.

Girls' 'borderlands' are certainly marginal to the adult, masculine and competition dominated systems of schooling, but my reading of margins is altogether more equivocal. Whilst girls' interpersonal relations are unquestionably 'other' to the rationalistic institution of schooling they are *not* unambiguously 'girl-friendly' nirvana. As the case studies make clear it has not been possible to write 'good news' sociology about resistant heroines. Writing the positive of girls' relations has also meant writing their conditions of division and difference. Writing their desires has also meant writing their envies, resentments; jealousies and oppressions (Kenway and Blackmore 1995).

Whilst schoolgirls' peer relations constituted an important alternative source of social definitions and social power, the affiliation systems operated *within* the gaze of hegemonic masculinity and the relations of class and race within which the dominant form arose. We need to acknowledge in other words that it is also 'in the margins' where girls' viciously normative e/valuations of each other are secured. My reading of 'girls' margins' suggests they offer more contradictory modes of identity than unadulterated oppositionality. I will return to this point. Next I consider the place of pleasure and desire in girls' groups.

Desiring girls

Schoolgirls' desiring economy of feminine friendship also stipulates microcultural variants of 'desired' places (Willis 1977; McRobbie 1978; Canaan 1986; Ashendon *et al.* 1987; Skeggs 1994). The theme of desire and the seeking of the desired place as a particular girl's friend recurs throughout the data. For example, Saskia's desire to be 'the boss' was bound up with and mediated by her attraction to Erin; Tamara's depiction of being chosen by one particular girl coded an intense moment of pleasure, as did the numerous confirmations of belonging to a group or to a particular girl. Just as it has been possible to interpret some of the girls' notes as 'hate mail' (case study 1), it is also possible to see others as 'love letters' (two Katies note).

Girls' relations certainly provided the necessary and minimum conditions for access to forms of acceptable sociality. They promised and frequently provided immediate rewards of prestige and popularity (company, fun, support, protection, advice, sociality), tokens which could not be conferred by school.[5] The 'best friend system', if you recall what Lois said, 'hangs heavily here' and as one of the main forms of friendship it offered modes of gratification against which the adult world of school could never hope to compete (Griffin 1985; Griffiths 1995). These unofficial and private forms conferred important if unofficial measures of social 'success'. Moreover girls in school moved between different 'desiring' systems. They occupied both the public world of schooling predicated on class determined modes of knowledge and academic success (Arnot 1982) and their own 'unofficial' prestige (desiring) systems. Some girls certainly accumulated public power from laying claim to the centre of the official value system (namely the élite groups in Eastford), but that did not provide immunity from their private struggles over the status as each other's friends, nor from their concerns about boyfriends nor even paradoxically from the pervasive pressures of seeking to fulfil desires and aspirations endorsed by schooling and parents.

Working-class girls had real difficulties in securing the 'preferred' place of schooling. However, not being able to achieve the place did not mean that those desires were simply liquidated or neutrally repositioned. Working-class girls' sense of rejection and disappointment needed active cultural management. Girlfriends were ideal for handling the pain of rejection. It was possible to identify two related cultural tactics.

Given that 'the typical girls' had little access to the 'good life' promised by academic compliance, they made sure that they could qualify for the more available forms of desirable identity as someone's girlfriend (see Skeggs 1994). A significant feature of their claim upon this position was shaped by a sexualized social antagonism against more privileged subjects (whether it was the élite girls – Suzy, Barbie and Lara – at Eastford, or Razia and the other 'boffins' at Crossfield).

Many of the most marginalized girls, the girls who were variously working-class, non-academic or truants, positioned 'other' girls as 'marginal' to what they themselves constructed as more important regimes of desire. Was it a form of class revenge to suggest that being a boffin was a contra-indication of success in the discourse of heterosexuality?[6]

As we have seen, 'typical girls' and 'no-hopers' (like Carol) turn towards the powerful (if deeply problematic and highly risky) positions in heterosexuality, always implying that they were in a place opposed and superior to the places of desire provided by schooling.[7] Heterosexuality and its practices was, at least in their aspirational dramas, 'other' and better since at some level it promised success (see McRobbie 1978 and Skeggs 1994 for a different view).

The investment of girls' relations by division and difference shaped by the category of (hetero)sexuality worked as one of the core cultural pre-occupations of girls' groups (see Griffiths's 1995 discussion of 'sameness' and 'difference'). I consider girls' social and sexual antagonism in some detail below.

Divide and rule

With little theoretical interest in, or empirical access to, the 'borderlands' (see Chapter 1 and 2) we have had little insight into how girls' private relations are indexed by power relations – or just how the public is lived through the private (Johnson 1986; Corrigan 1987; Griffin 1995). Margaret Atwood's heroine, and the subjects of this ethnography, re-mind us incessantly of girls' alliances as microtechnologies of power which function so effectively because of their uniquely invisible and intimate nature.

All the girls in the study had to confront the abiding structuring re-ality of masculine fear of their sexual autonomy. This (along with school-ing) organized girls' social worlds. Differences of class amongst the girls altered rather than eradicated the persistent peer, community and famil-ial hunt for signs of inappropriate sexual identity. Jude and her friends, for example, were continuously regulated by masculine authority within their various communities, and they in turn produced accounts of their own and 'other' girls' behaviour through the categories of surveillance (bad image, looked hard, the other side of the hill).

Middle-class girls had more material (and sexual) freedom but they too were regulated by bourgeois cultural protocols about 'excess' or fears of sexual non-conformity. These fears were dramatized through the contradictory sexual meanings given to Barbie's style when she wore her suit (see Chapter 7). They were also displayed in how Suzy, Lara and Barbie read working-class girls' sexual style as an 'abnormality' or as an excess of heterosexuality – 'jailbait' as one of them told me. Working-class girls, according to this discourse, were over-feminized. This was, as we have noted, a neat inversion of working-class girls' coding of middle classness as lack of femininity ('boffin').

These are cultural equations in which the structuring effects of class relations (lived at schooling level ostensibly and officially as academic competitiveness) are culturally transformed and lived at the vernacular level from within both dominant and subordinate class positions simul-taneously as sexual denigration and competition. Here is what Foucault (1980) has called a 'microphysics' of power – and the only boys in sight are those 'in the head' (Holland *et al.* 1991).

Research into the borderlands has above all else therefore shown girls' transgressive desires, their subordinated knowledges (Corrigan 1987) as highly contradictory because they are inflected through girls' differently invested relations to homosociality, schooling, class, community and heterosexuality. We can recollect Amelia's affinity to, as well as policing of, her relationship to Gabbie; Sally and Jude's 'transgressive text' capitulating to 'normality'; the two Katies' necessary recourse to the language of 'hygienic motherhood'; the class privileged 'semi-feminism' of Suzy (McRobbie and McCabe 1981:20); the problematic bossiness of Saskia; and the semi-feminist 'common sense' of Jude and her friends as well as their racist misogyny.

It is only possible to locate such split and fractured data through an analysis of the wider social divisions of power condensed; co-constructed and carried there. The following section explores how these wider networks of power variously propose the 'normal'. It is by tracking the recursive features of girls' friendship as sites of sameness, as boundaries against difference, that we can locate them in a social architecture of hegemony.

'Becoming normal, becoming a girl': reflections on hegemonic masculinity

Understanding girls' intimate friendship demands paradoxically that we have to understand the social force of hegemonic masculinity. Paradigmatically it is the prevailing politics of normative gender difference (girls and boys as opposite sexes) which provides the terms through which girls' ideological and material segregation from boys continually produces girls' same-sex relationships as well as their sexual and social pathologization.

These social tensions are dramatized most intensely through the re-positioning of the distinctive cultural forms of girls as friends (physical proximity, secrecy, intimacy and exclusiveness) as part of a 'symbolic political language' (Edelman 1971) of 'heterosexual hegemony' (see Lees 1986; Hey 1988, 1994). The retells about 'the lesbian rumours' concerning Suzy, Lara and Barbie (and numerous other girls) indicate the pervasive power of the 'male gaze' (Rossiter 1994) to seek out even those spaces which by their very definition are girl only (see later).

If girls are unavoidably complicit with the overwhelming logics of hegemonic gender narratives, this is partly because of a lack of a *collective* consciousness/language. After all girls had little sustained access to a public 'symbolic political language' capable of reflecting on what it is that is common or shared about their subordinated positioning within the terms of hegemonic masculinity (Arnot 1982).

On the contrary, the formal pedagogy of schooling was about denying questions of differences to their subjects (Walkerdine 1985). There was little official encouragement to engage school students in discussions of the divisions and relations of power. It is not surprising therefore to find that these relations are consistently reanimated within the margins when girls conspicuously appear to invest each other through the 'differences' and divisions of power they live within.

It is here I think that we can locate the 'natural' tendency for girls to institute their friendships through the categories of 'sameness' as 'normality' and against 'difference' as 'other', which has been commented on by many social researchers (Lever 1976; Llewellyn 1980; Rubin 1980; Griffiths 1995). It is *only* denaturalized if it is seen that such investments promise a major cultural resource capable of handling the contradictions that schooling both expresses and then denies (see Arnot 1982 and Walkerdine 1985).

Girlfriends provide the key to social inclusion or exclusion. Furthermore belonging generated class meanings about what it meant to be a girl. There are impressive affinities of the working-class girls Gabbie and Amelia 'stuck together'; Iris and Sonia's account of Erin's clique as 'not our sort of girl'; Gina's downwardly mobile shift into 'becoming one of the girls' against the grain of her father's aspirations. Even the dissidents, here I am thinking of Carol's homosocial isolation as well as Saskia's upwardly mobile but spectacularly unsuccessful bid for Erin's friendship, took place against a background of the intensities and presumption of girlhood friendship – the 'female world of love and ritual' in Smith-Rosenberg's phrase (1975:1).

If belonging was the name of the game, then being accepted implied the performing of appropriate forms of femininity. The words of Barbie resonate at this point: 'I didn't want to be classed as one of them'. Girls' practices, in other words, had as their major aim the making of feminine identity or reputation through the axis of conformity to classed sexual codes. Examples like 'being improved' abound, being transformed into a 'slag' or otherwise surveyed – tactics which were made available by girls' unique capacity to 'get beneath each other's skin' by establishing powerful judgements upon the surfaces of each others' bodies.

The microcultural politics of girls' homosociality were therefore steeped in co-appraisals. Girls insisted on making each other into acceptable selves, in 'suitable' appearances and dispositions (variously caring, nice, kind, attractive, confiding but not too close), positions and predispositions which went right to the heart of how girls were supposed to perform their roles as each other's friends in conditions controlled by forms of hegemonic masculinity (Connell 1987, 1995; Griffiths 1995).

Moreover concerns about appearance do not discriminate at one level. We had Suzy's hating of her body; Barbie's confidence rocked by the 'dyke' label; Jude and Gina's bitchy assassinations of the River Bridge gang; Saskia's put-down as a 'heterosexual reject'; the working-class girls' critique of the élite as 'hippies' and the élite's converse critique of them as 'tarty'. Carol's pleasure about her physical appearance is unique. The girls in my study therefore, despite their differences, could not avoid the superordinate intense scrutiny of hegemonic masculine culture. In very many respects they did the work of that culture amongst and between themselves in positioning each other into particular places (Walkerdine 1981; Davies 1989). Alison Jones has asked that:

> Researchers take an interest in the processes through which girls 'correctly' position themselves in available discourses including the *sanctions against particular positions and encouragement towards others which could vary across and within class, and race, culture and discursive context.*
>
> (Jones 1993:162, my emphasis)

It was only through recognizing the core social resources of girls' friendship economies – talking, note writing, gossiping, bitching, bantering, and parody – that it was possible to access some discursive and social means of persuasion and dissuasion.

Alison Jones (1993), like others before her, has drawn attention to the differences between middle-class and working-class girls. She comments however, that there is an overwhelming tendency for positions to be coordinated through dominant gender narratives. She identifies the powerful coalition between dominant gender 'scripts' and girls' own desire to be 'normal' as crucial. My own discovery of girls' investment in 'insider femininity' (good) in opposition to other girls' 'outsider femininity' (bad) (see McRobbie 1978; Llewellyn 1980) resounds here. Girls' common experiences of sexual division and domination did not in short generate gender solidarity. Girls' occupation of, and insertion into cross-cutting multiple regimes of power (Anyon 1983; hooks 1992; Jones 1993) constructed identifications *against* as opposed to *with* other girls. It is only through theorizing struggles *between* girls as embodying/embodied forms of cultural and material power that we can connect the networks of supposedly private forms of subjectivity and identity to the making of cultural hegemony.

This reading has proposed that different troupes of girls and individual girls within those troupes are respectively empowered, disenfranchised, evaluated, re/evaluated, encultured, or 'improved' within and through their contestation of numerous 'desired' places. These places are variously distributed within the regimes of schooling, homosociality and heterosexuality. In sum there is a public 'school address' to girls, ostensibly asexual (Walkerdine 1981; 1985; 1986) but highly heterosexualized in practice (Epstein 1995), and a variety of privately appropriated (classed, racialized, culturally specific) 'girls' addresses' to each other. Both public and private realms generated distinct discursive frameworks in the form of a matrix of disciplinary forms of power, namely 'normalization' (Foucault 1977:182) and 'surveillance' (Foucault 1977:216; Gore 1995).

Girls' investments in meanings and practices derived within girlfriendship signified much more than can be referenced through either the imprecise notion of the 'hidden curriculum' or the glamourized notion of margins. We have been made aware for example of the scope of the cultural work undertaken as the social 'contracts' of friendship: Saskia's exclusion; Sally's liminality; Jude's group's disinvestment in schooling; some élite girls' construction of class; other working-class girls' counter-constructions of racialized and classed forms of sexuality as well as various girls' abiding fear of their own intimate modes of relating to each other.

From the outset it is crucial to recognize the extent of the subordinating social and cultural pressures that confront girls. It is only through acknowledging the elusive and opaque criteria of formal schooling, let alone the obtuse and flatly contradictory meanings about femininity proposed by hegemonic masculinity, that we can come to understand what is at stake for girls if they 'dare to be different'. The problem faced by girls is how they are to become simultaneously a 'normal' schoolgirl and 'a proper young woman' within the respective cultural institutions of (compulsory) schooling and (compulsory) heterosexuality.[8] One institution *denies* difference whilst the other is fundamentally invested in *producing* it, so that femininity as sexual difference under terms of subordination is always in play against masculinity in dominance. The difficulty for girls is that of seeking out empowering places within regimes alternately committed to denying subordination or celebrating it (Coward 1984; Griffin 1985; Walkerdine 1986).

It is precisely the lack of powerful *public* discourses for different groups of girls that potentiates the significance of girls' *private* relations with each other. As Amelia so eloquently put it, 'I'm stuck with her and whether she likes it or not she's stuck with me'.

It is girls' experience of 'differences' that are incessantly displaced or denied by the centre that overdetermines girls' need for 'other' girls as a way to make sense of their own identity.[9] They are almost compelled to position themselves *against* girls who appear to be what they are not. We have seen girls endlessly exercised as each other's critics and self-regulators by the search for compliance with numerous gender, class (and race) specific dimensions of 'normality'. 'Becoming normal' therefore was intimately tied in with their pleasure in acting as each others' mirrors, confidantes and minders of shared cultural understandings as classed female subjects. Since both working-class and middle-class cliques were monitored through familial and community-inspired patriarchal and class-specific ideologies and practices, these groups then turned both *in* upon each other and *out* towards 'the other' seeking to find the right way to be 'normally' hetero *and* sexual (or appropriately/normally 'clever' or a 'laugh' or 'nice').[10]

If it is true that girls, as Griffin (1994:5) says, have 'to be "won" to heterosexuality', we have to understand that such 'winning' necessarily has to be secured through forms of 'normalization' implemented through and sustained within girls' relations. Stuart Hall's (1992:16) account of difference as the product of 'distributive relations' captures the dialectical 'economy of othering' that I am striving to describe:

> Contrary to the superficial evidence, there is nothing simple about the structures and dynamics of racism . . . It is racism's very rigidity that is due to its complexity. Its capacity to punctuate the universe into two great opposites masks something else; it masks the complexes of feelings and attitudes, beliefs and conceptions, that are always refusing to be so neatly stabilized and fixed. . . . All the symbolic and narrative energy and work is directed to secure us 'over here' and them 'over there', to fix each in its appointed species place. It is a way of masking how deeply our histories actually intertwine and interpenetrate; how necessary 'the Other' is to our own sense of identity; how even the dominant, colonizing, imperializing power only knows who and what it is and can only experience the pleasure of its own power of domination in and through the construction of the Other.[11]

If we seek to connect the cultural more firmly with the psychic structuring of identity Valerie Walkerdine's (1987) work offers us one way of stating that connection. She has proposed that the exclusion of femininity from claims to positions of power results in girls experiencing femininity as a series of psychic splits. She argues for example, how difficult it is for girls to occupy the 'opposed' positions of 'being feminine' and 'being clever': 'No wonder that some of us split them apart in various ways or have different conscious and unconscious methods for dealing with the unbearable contradiction' (Walkerdine 1987:277). Her related work on power and desire (1985) offers a way to think about the psychic investments which young girls bring to their identifications with more powerful others. She describes girls as struggling to obtain power through an identification with their female teacher. This calls for both active suppression of conflict as well as projection of 'horridness' onto boys, in order that girls can lay claim to the position of 'niceness'.

Walkerdine's psychic economy model cannot however, account for how girls are also invested in the (seductive) and powerful positions proposed by heterosexuality. In broad terms, the ethnography shows that investments into 'the desired place' of heterosexuality entailed 'projections' which could only 'work' when dispersed amongst girls.

Such evidence further complicates understanding of these processes. 'Being nice' as other writers argue, is *specific* to the formulation of white middle class femininity (Jones 1993; Griffin 1995; Kenway and Blackmore 1995). The social aspiration to be 'nice' was mainly taken up by the middle-class white girls (see Chapters 4 and 7). Saskia was rejected by her middle-class friends because, as one of them put it, 'She was not as nice as she was supposed to be'.

Most of the working-class girls in the study expressed less an invest-ment in powerful female others than an investment in powerful male others. Here they sought out 'niceness' as a form of sexual etiquette about 'allowing men near enough' (see also Hey 1988). 'Niceness' for Jude's group was therefore more a (racialized) dating protocol than any search for power through identification with a teacher. Similarly Carol's rejection of bourgeois 'niceness' was about her recognition that such 'niceness' represented infantilization and desexualization. Her own ver-sion of 'looking nice' was explicitly concerned with making the most of her sexual assets, as was the intervention into her friend's dress sense.

We have seen these cultural and psychic logics mapped through the dimensions of either class, sex or race (and sometimes all at once). The élite were the élite because they were not the un-nice 'fishwives'. 'Hetero-sex' was always something that an/*other* girl was doing, never you; black girls were 'oversexed'; Asian girls were 'undersexed', whilst the white working-class femininity Jude and her friends constructed was just right – just sexy enough. In Maureen's case we remember that she did not so much split herself from (sexual) desires through projecting them onto African-Caribbean boys (this was precisely what was forbidden cultur-ally) but recruited her friends into projecting them with intense racist misogyny onto 'other' white girls (see Chapter 5) and more obliquely invested the sexual identity of African-Caribbean girls with fantasies of rapaciousness and excess.

We have discussed the salience of Maureen's role as 'ventriloquizing' these wider cultural forms for her group. We have the evidence of girls' sense of self as being constantly under review by the compelling pres-sures of familial and community forms of control; the normalizing voice of Gina's father in her account; Jude and Gina celebrating but ultimately circumscribing their own pleasure in being 'bad girls' through heed-ing the hectoring voices of other girls. The ever present but absent 'voice in the head' of dominant normative ideologies of white working-class masculinity acts as a constant source of surveillance, bringing girls to heel.

The struggle for meeting the criteria of popular definitions of 'normal-ity' takes on particular force for those girls denied access to dominant forms of cultural and social power – to what Corrigan (1987:38) has called 'a desire to be in "those places" so designated, so approved'. Jude's group's microcultural practices were to a large extent reworkings of a script of 'normality'/'common sense' proposed by their host (racist/ sexist) community cultures. Becoming 'normal' meant in effect appeasing this culture through making cultural proposals at the cost of their own, as well as other girls', sexual and social freedom and autonomy.

Hall's (1992) metaphor of 'symbolic and narrative energy' and Walkerdine's account of psychic investment allows us to appreciate the density and the multilayered nature of the social, cultural and personal resources which have to be mobilized by girl subjects in their effort to secure their place in the midst of contradictory 'ways to be'. The utility of girls as each other's guarantors of appropriate identity proclaims a social process that also and inadvertently maintains the normative fictions of gender, race and class (Walkerdine 1987, 1990).

We have some trenchant indications of how girls' struggle to retain positions of power *as* and within difference. We have documented girls splitting 'other' girls from claims to heterosexual femininity; from claims to 'niceness'; from the place of desirability as either a friend or as a girlfriend – all of these cultural efforts invest belonging as the ability to exercise exclusion. The ruptures girls enact represent *as well as activate* the lived differences of class and race. It is after all the evaluation of other girls in terms of their 'performance of friendship' as a 'performance of femininity' which organizes the moral and social economy of girls' relations.

Girls made this moral and social economy out of the interplay of discourses – of being 'nice', of being a 'good girl' or of being 'one of the girls'. These discourses converge around a common investment in proposing the desired place as 'normal' and the despised and feared place of the other as 'abnormal' (Walkerdine 1985, 1986; Jones 1993). In other words, are you one of us or one of them? It would seem that just as 'differences' are the inescapable terms through which we come to locate ourselves as a subject (Bhabba 1990; Hall 1991, 1992; Epstein 1993), the flip side of our culture's attempts to keep those differences mattering (as the relations of subordination and domination) are those incessant invitations to construct the binaries of 'normality/abnormality' and the boundaries between them. Girls, as we have seen, are heavily involved in making their friendship as a vernacular version of 'being normal'. What's more, the place of 'normality' can *only* be understood through its opposite – as the place *not* to be or, more accurately, as the *girl* not to be (Campbell 1993; Griffiths 1995).

Walkerdine's suggestion that we seek to displace our 'badness'/ab/ normalities through forms of projection whilst originating as a psychological construct, is also sociologically compelling. If girls are endlessly drawn within regimes which seek to subject them to 'impossible places', we can locate the particular utility of girls as friends and as enemies.[12]

The 'bad' can be offloaded, culturally speaking, onto those others outside of the desired place of self. We should not be at all surprised that the pre-existing hierarchies of domination and subordination are themselves constantly reanimated by the social and psychic dynamics of different girls as they seek a powerful place from which to speak.

Furthermore, we can locate the particular effectivity of girls' exclusive best friendships here, as an attempt to find just one such powerful place. Within my study, for example, locked inside the broader based groups of girls were best-friendship dyads (Jude and Gina; Erin and Samantha). Such bonds functioned as bottom line arbiters, co-conspirators or simple reflectors who could confirm each other safe inside their self-reflecting world of the other as 'same'. A girl's best friend is her best friend because here (at least theoretically) girls can find the reflection of a self-confirmed as 'normal' since the face that smiles back is our friend/ourself.

I would suggest that what is invested in friendship practices is the attempt to inscribe the subject into a position which suppresses or directs desire and difference. The fate of two contrasting 'outsider' girls is relevant here. Carol's semi-detached position was after all born out of her calculation that playing 'hyper femininity' in school was simply not worth the boredom. Like 'Snail' (Llewellyn 1980), Carol transgressed that bit too far to be tolerated by either her friends, teachers and eventually by her family. Saskia's challenge was in a different way equally threatening to the stabilities of meanings attached to what it meant to be 'properly' feminine, nice and middle-class. She was expelled from her group and also coincidentally semi-detached from her family by going to boarding school. Even Suzy's 'cleverness' was seen to be a marked category and as destabilizing by her erstwhile friend.

Girls have to make sense of themselves *against* other girls but they have to do so not in conditions of their own choosing. We can locate some of the features of girls' relations here. We have seen girls' longings for certain girls, for a sense of belonging to certain groups, and argued that these affinities resonate as another politics of 'desire' played out in the inclusions and exclusions of personal forms of feminine intimacies (see Steedman 1986:33).[13] There is however more to it than that. Not only were 'places' desired, they were loathed, not only wanted, they were repudiated. Moreover, given that the 'places' were *embodied* by 'other' girls and all they represented – looks, clothes, manners, forms of sexual self display or 'cleverness' – we should not be too surprised to discover that the various economies of girls' friendships carried both intense sources of personal affiliation as well as forms of social antagonism.

There are numerous implications of this data both at the level of theory, pedagogy and feminist educational politics. I want simply to concentrate on one major theme of this study – the politics of language – in this final section because it allows me to draw together elements from all three concerns.

Discourse and difference: girls' talk and the politics of language

As we have seen, the significance of *difference* in girls' relationships is highly complex and contradictory. Whilst it has been acknowledged that friendship groups are most likely to be constituted from peers who share a similar background, it is also important to acknowledge the variability and fluidities within girls' groups. It is precisely through mapping the shifts in alliances that one can access the ways in which difference is made to matter. Furthermore different differences signify in different contexts and at different times. Through recording how differences emerge one can begin to identify how regulation is brought into play and by whom and with what effect.

We have numerous instances: Maureen's 'ventriloquism' of racism; Suzy's role in mobilizing a puritan form of feminism; Barbie's mother's role in surveying her sexual identity and self-presentation; Natalie and Anna's joint punishment of Saskia by invoking her failed (hetero)-sexuality; and Jude's group's role in bringing the aspirations of her friend Gina under control. These are key discursive moments in attempts to 'fix' what it means to be a girl or to be a particular sort of girl.

This study suggests the crucial importance of language and discourse as constructing 'permissible' places from which to speak. We urgently need to interrogate which forms of discourse create what sort of places and how these positions encode cultural and social powers for their speakers and forms of powerlessness for those silenced (Frazer and Cameron 1989).

Bakhtin's theorization of the dialogic nature of ideology (see Barker 1989; Wertsch 1991) can provide us with a way into understanding how 'direct, face-to-face, vocalized verbal communication between persons' (Voloshinov 1993:95) ' "interanimates" the utterance of another' (Wertsch 1991:54).[14] Self-evidently the social relations of cultural hegemony and their contestation are implicated in the speech genres and discourses mobilized by girls (see Ashendon *et al.* 1987:253). The power of 'distant voices' has after all echoed throughout this book, the inheritance of familial, cultural and community discourse which is reworked in girls' ever present dense cultural 'interanimations' or 'ventriloquisms'. We can 'hear' the white working-class brothers, boyfriends and fathers of the Crossfield girls; the domineering adults in Carol's life; the judgemental familial repertoires of working-class mothers; middle-class mothers and teachers.

Girls' private/social relations are however also at a distance from the public/social world of schooling and this makes for at least a double axis to forms of public discourse and power. We have seen the numerous productivities of their *own* talk. There are samples of solidarity through social disclosing and sharing (Griffiths 1995) as well as evidence of cultural forms which seem to fit the description of chaos/freedom (Scheurich 1995), excluding and dividing 'othering' talk, and parodies and subversions in addition to complicities and betrayals.

Whilst many commentators have noted the role of talk in the construction of feminine forms of intimacy, few have understood its role in constructing divisions. What is called for is a recognition of the complicity of vernacular knowledges with hegemonic forms of knowledge – vernacular forms/different knowledge which Corrigan (1987:23) has identified as redolent 'in a thousand quiet, implicit, prismatic forms [which] does become communicated through particular social relations. It makes up the dense texture of social life, part of a social economy'.

I would suggest that it is because we have so little understanding about the provenance and status of the complexes of 'vernacular knowledges' held by subjects that there has been a tendency to assume a one-sided and romanticized view of their output. These structured absences speak to the need for a renewal of interest into the sociology of schooling cultures and the role of discourses in their production. Frazer and Cameron point us in this direction: 'Social researchers must pay more attention to the question of what practices there are and who participates in which' (1989:33). Certainly girls' notes worked both as 'illegitimate knowledges' (Prendergast and Prout 1980:529) and as 'vernacular literacies' (Camitta 1993). Girls' capacities to call up these knowledges represented considerable gendered cultural capital circulating amongst and across girls' groups. It is, as I have argued *because* girls encode meanings and provide forms of understanding in the so-called private domain which makes recognition of their power difficult and intervention in their circuits highly problematic.[15]

We need to reauthorize our understanding of the culture of civil society in the private as well as the public. If we shift towards the material cultural practices of gossip, school yard chatter and the social relations of peers – the domains where we have seen the circulation of informal knowledges (counter-knowledges or transgressive texts) – we are more able to see the social processes involved in the construction of a pupil self. Here we are on the terrain of the social etiquettes and conventions of place – on the 'borderlands' with their own borderlands (Steedman 1986; Epstein 1993). Here are some of the means through which the social exclusions and inclusions of pupil social life are mapped and lived. Here we have pupil subjects who belong to 'our group' as opposed to 'the other'; to specific classes and races; to sexualities that are proper as opposed to being the other side of the hill. We have also parody, defiance, ostensible compliance but resistance, disguise and dissembling (Corrigan 1988), 'passing' (Kuhn 1995, Chapter 6), solidarity and self-protection, and above all else the persistent (if highly contradictory) existence of girls' homosocial alliances.

In occupying this conceptual space we have a way to think about how some girl subjects take up their own place in the culture through the conduit of intimacy (see Davies 1984; Thorne 1993). A measure of girls' resistance is their insistence on friendship but the fact that it takes the form that it does reveals the extent to which as a social form it carries the weight of girls' general subordination within schooling and masculine culture (Cockburn 1986).

In a sense nothing is surprising about identifying the 'offstage' as the site for girls' technologies of power. Rowbotham (1973) spoke about a 'women's lore' transmitted through 'personal' talk. Jones (1980) has argued that female 'gossip' is a 'specific type of women's "language" or style' representing the outcome of a particular 'speech community'. It originates in settings which are 'characterized by restriction. The private, the personal domain . . . is the cultural setting' (Jones 1980:194).

If we consider girls' notes we have numerous fascinating precedents. Smith-Rosenberg has spoken of the 'passionate' attachments affirmed in the correspondence of nineteenth-century upper-class American women as the 'female world of love and ritual' (Smith-Rosenberg 1975). Minolin (1986) writes of the existence of 'secret women's writing'. Ann Oakley (1974:15) drew attention to the role of 'gossip as a form of unarticulated female power'. Gluckman (1963:307) provided an anthropological perspective that, despite being ungendered, cited gossip and scandal as 'among the most important societal and cultural phenomena we are called upon to study'. He describes the function of gossip variously as: working to discipline social relations through providing checks on excessive individualism, selecting leaders and controlling aspiring individuals and cliques. In other words it represents a social strategy strongly motivated by the desire for uniformity amongst group members. The relevance of this characterization of 'gossip' to the previous argument will, I hope, be self-evident.

As we have seen, girls' 'gossip' and 'scandal' is organized by their quest to 'become normal'. Furthermore it has only been possible to provide an analytic focus upon the apparently random, diverse and multiple cultural practices of different troupes of girls through locating girls' talk both within and as in part constituting relations of power *and* powerlessness. This account has analysed the making of white girl subjects in terms of the connections of the individual (and her friends) to a whole matrix of regulatory practices – of schooling as an institution and to the cultural privileging of middle-class values and whiteness which it enforces. Here it has been claimed that girls' social relations ('compulsory homosociality') were lived through the co-investment in forms of 'normality' mandated by the hegemonic cultural formula of 'compulsory heterosexuality' (Rich 1980) or 'hetero-reality' (Raymond 1986).[16]

If we have not been surprised by finding girls' talk reflecting and constituting hegemonic narratives, we need to bear in mind that it offered cultural resources of counter-hegemony as well. This signifies that we need to work *with* as well as *against* its cultural power. Hall's (1990: 225) remarks about the incomplete nature of identity are well taken:

> Cultural identity . . . is a matter of 'becoming' as well as 'being'. It belongs to the future as much as the past. It is not something which already exists, transcending place, time, history and culture . . . identities are the names we give to the different ways we are positioned by, and position ourselves within, the narratives of the past.

The neglect of the personal modes of culture has kept the specific feminine practices of girlhood friendship confined to the margins – untheorized, unseen and unresearched. However if it is the 'structured absence' of friendship which acts as a mirror for the social 'performances' of girls' gender, we are required both to continue to theorize how it works and think through how we might acknowledge its social importance and its cultural significance.

The women's movement's early look at the personal aspects of oppression, privileged consciousness-raising as one way to explore connections between lived private forms and the social divisions of sex. It was an attempt to identify and then to change what Richard Johnson has called (in another context) 'the condescensions of the powerful and the secrecies of the oppressed' (1986:287–8).

We have returned to other forms of these relations in this book. We have had to consider both forms of oppression produced through sexual divisions and, perhaps from a feminist point of view even more problematic, forms of power produced as socially antagonistic divisions/differences *between* girls. In sum, if it is against other girls that girls seek to measure themselves in the first instance, then we are compelled to think about how to interrupt/interrogate and engage girls in a critique of precisely those comparisons which are experienced as privately lived moments of social and sexual competitiveness. Our question is not so much Judith Williamson's (1981/2)spoof question, 'How does girl number twenty understand ideology?' as how can we create a feminist politics of education that takes account of the claim that girl number 20 comes to be understood *herself* in ideology against girl number 21. Within classrooms we will have, as Sandra Taylor argues, the 'lived social relations [of girls] and these relations are part of what she calls 'a network of meanings which constitute the social world and which may be viewed as a series of sites of struggle over meaning' (Taylor 1993:127).

The issue is how to both recognize girls' systems of connection without pathologizing them, how to disrupt their circuiting of difference (in terms of racism, classism and homophobia) and how to reposition their transgressive forms more firmly as critical resources and repositories which can make new versions of good sense – forms which could potentially consolidate their proto-feminist circlings of boys and men as invested in making them subjects within subordination.

Notes

1 It is self-evident that these were moments in subjects' histories and biographies and taken from particular social fragments. The theoretical claims I am making are highly speculative and could well be modified through other studies of different groups of girls in different sites and locations. Nevertheless, despite different configurations, the general themes of girls as enmeshed in the homosocial institution of girl friendship I take as something which will hold true across sites and groups.

2 Throughout the book my interpretation of the case studies has confronted and then sought to explain *how* hegemony has been installed (or resisted) precisely through processes obscured in the 'backstage' (see Elias 1978) 'back regions' world of girls' privatized 'identity work'.

  As we have seen, girls' notes played an important part in these cultural transmissions (the two Katies note; Saskia's exclusion; the transgressive letter between Sally and Jude), as did gossip (especially the role of rumour in policing behaviour, for example, the élite trio and the lesbian 'scare'. We have a repertoire of different forms of talk as well as other forms of communication: bantering, chatting, miming, the use of secret codes, toilet graffiti, letters and phone calls, in sum a multitude of social transactions.

3 This expression comes from a review of Linda Williams's (1988) essay on the film *A Question of Silence*. Beverley Skeggs comments that 'the film visualises the wild zone of women's culture which is not spoken but experienced' (Skeggs 1991:264).

4 Analogous to this we can suggest that the cultural positioning of heterosexuality as *the* form of socially sanctioned sexual identity continues to regulate/ seduce in spite of schooling's deliberately desexed public texts equating sexuality with marital biological reproduction. Evasions and mystifications merely incite rather than overrule counter-investments in the making of (hetero)sexuality.

5 Interpersonal sanctions were equally transparent and immediate: being 'sent to Coventry', rude letters, exclusions, rumours, graffiti.

6 This disqualification in its term probably contributes to the older élite girls' determination not to be seen as 'bluestockings' (see Richards forthcoming) and might explain Barbie's own serial relationships with numerous boys as a form of 'hyper femininity'.

7 See Hey (1988) for a more detailed exploration of the sexual politics of Jude's group. In the schooling context the girls could only be positioned as childlike, controlled, failed and relatively powerless.

8 If you are working-class or black these positions are likely to be experienced as even more contradictory or unattainable since one has also been confronted by different culturally specific practices and definitions (Mirza 1992). This is also true for girls with disabilities (Griffin 1995).

9 Valerie Walkerdine writes that the condition for the production of the rational, self-regulating bourgeois subject is that difference is displaced and the workings of power denied (1985).

10 The connective significance of Barbie being almost as subordinated as Carol by her boyfriends is relevant here as is the similar pressure on Gina to give up on academic work and on Suzy to stop being so clever.

11 There is a specific history of racism(s) which cannot be collapsed into other forms of relations of domination and subordination – but since girls in the study, not only patterned 'othering' as racial difference but also as class difference, Hall's model is useful in understanding how the girls appear to locate their own femininity on the terrain of 'an/other' which equally 'masks' as well as requires multiple regimes of 'interdependencies' and 'connections'.

12 Hudson (1984) cites a girl as saying, 'Whatever we do, it is always wrong'.

13 Like Bronwyn Davies, my account of desire includes, rather than being confined to, the erotic. It incorporates the desires produced within the material and ideological settings of 'consumption', especially those material longings for particular forms of embodiment and social success (see Walkerdine 1990:89; Davies 1993).

14 Barker glosses 'interanimation' thus: 'We take hold of someone else's talk and embed it in our own' (1989:269). Participation in dialogue implies that we orient ourselves to the propositions of another's speech and that we are able to create our own propositions. By implementing orientations (evaluative accents) we 'position it'. Parody for example, is about *re*positioning content and instituting a different sort of discourse – through applying a different evaluative accent than the one originally granted. It is interesting to consider the role of parody as subversion in girls' notes.

15 'They don't say any of the things they say in front of others, even other children: whatever is going on is going on in secret, among the four of us only. Secrecy is important' (Atwood 1990:120).

16 'Compulsory homosociality' is freely adopted from Rich (1980).

EPILOGUE

As the Acknowledgements indicated, writing this book has not been easy – the result of the 'speed up' conditions which pass for academic life. Additionally it has been a challenge to find a form which can hold the subjectivities of the girls at the same time as theorize them. In seeking a reconciliation between academic narration and girls' voices I have inevitably sacrificed aspects of the emotional and social complexities as well as the spontaneities of girls' friendship dramas.

Having done my best to render the dynamically inconsistent 'other' into the less pliable genre of sociological abstraction, it is hard to let go of text and subjects in the form of this book. I am aware that the resultant production does not and cannot represent what it is I want it to. Language is recalcitrant. The move to 'let the subject drop' was eventually made in this case by accepting that interpretations are always provisional and partial. This is not therefore the new truth about how girls' friendship works. However it is at this point that a contradiction emerges. Gearing up to write did involve a stake in a related claim – I certainly do not want to modulate my conviction that what I have to say is of some importance. If we are interested in strengthening a feminist politics of education we need to recognize the rawness of the informal cultures girls make in schools rather than rely on uncorroborated fantasies about how we would wish them to be.

There is a further irony – namely that just when I am revisiting the truculent data on which my argument relies there are on general release some highly seductive claims about 'the transformation of intimacy' (Giddens 1993). Giddens contends that feminism allied with technological, demographic and economic change have converged to create conditions within which individuals can free themselves from the rigidities of binary gender categories and their associated oppressive relations and relationships. The emergence of 'plastic' sexualities – of femininities un-hooked from reproduction – presages the emergence of democratized intimacy, creating the forms of social engagement which liberate children from tyrannical parents, women from unfeeling husbands and subjects from the presumptions of heterosexuality. According to the argument we are invited into the Utopia of late modernity, a post-feminist 'Identities R Us' where we can theoretically shop around for forms of self that best suit our particular social, sexual and relational aspirations. Derived from a study of secondary sources (popular self-help manuals), Giddens's optimistic vision is a long way from Jude and Carol's world and the decidedly more robust forms of normative selves proposed by class and racialized friendships.

Social forms have undoubtedly freed up and yet I do not think that what I captured was the last throw of the dice in the old game of binary certainties – when girls were girls and the pursuit of the 'normal' was all-consuming. The viciousness of the racism and the classed forms of social and sexual antagonism was deeply embedded within girls' wider social networks. I do not think that the majority of the girls would have moved on to invent more 'plastic selves' after I left the field. In other words, claims of change need specifying empirically and are, I would suggest, generation and class as well as gender specific. Young girls after all are about making themselves at a time of acute bodily/social transfiguration and are concerned about 'fitting in'. More fundamentally, deconstructing a self requires that you first manufacture one.

Giddens's claims are, as he recognizes, to some extent culturally specific. One needs the power to imagine and rework both a self and a future; it requires time, aspiration, resources, ambition, energy and confidence. These social resources are differentially distributed amongst social groups and whilst they might well be available to metropolitan smarties they show little sign of being 'socialized', thus enabling the majority to join in.

It is salutary to return to the empirical material furnished for this book and to note how power is not so much transformed as intimately refurbished. When girls relate to each other they do so through the public certainties and structures of class, race and gender. If this is my argument then neither the blandishments of simplistic equal opportunities appeals to unspecified girls that 'girls rule okay' nor the tempting assertions of late modernity (as the desire to democratize intimacy) can adequately formulate an effective political address that can work with as well as undercut the empirical data I have presented. Contemporary evidence of the existence of so-called 'girl gangs' (ITV, *The Tuesday Special*, November 1995) intent upon extreme forms of 'othering' suggest that there is rather more dividing and ruling going on than democratic transfigurative practices.

It isn't that I want to be curmudgeonly and perversely downbeat, but the pull of the data allied with contemporary concerns about fragmenting and disenfranchised communities tells an altogether more awkward story. More specifically we have in the course of this book encountered narratives of 'imperfect' selves as the girls search for coherence in their imperfect worlds. Undoubtedly some (like Suzy) may have gone on to become the heroines of self actualization and maybe other girls are 'doing it for themselves' – if so, great. It is also true, however, that to a large extent we cannot answer these questions because we haven't got the empirical research on which to base our understandings.

Furthermore, work that is concerned with investigating the making of subjectivities in conditions of cultural change (Gordon 1995) is undertaken in a climate of indifference or hostility to equity or social justice issues. Policy makers and politicians (at least in England around education) are entranced by macrolevel analysis of school performance. The gaze is now so well away from ethnographies and smaller qualitative work that children's experience of schooling is in danger of being equated with their standardized test results or GCSE mean scores.

Interesting developments in Australia point towards areas of work which speak to the implications of my study, work that recognizes the importance of the privatized and private domain, work on the role of emotions and subjectivity in education that complicates debates about how best to construct pedagogies making for effective educational interventions around gender (Kenway and Blackmore 1995). I see my own work as contributing towards this through the making of what Carolyn Steedman calls, in a related context, 'a structure of political thought that will take all of this, all these secret and impossible stories, recognize what has been made out on the margins, and then, recognizing it, refuse to celebrate it' (1986:144).

REFERENCES

Alcoff, L. (1988) Cultural feminism versus post-structuralism: the identity crisis in feminist theory. *Signs: Journal of Women in Culture and Society*, 13(3):405–36.

Anyon, J. (1983) Intersections of gender and class: accommodation and resistance by working class and affluent females to contradictory sex role ideologies, in S. Walker and L. Barton (eds) *Gender, Class and Education*. London: Falmer Press.

Arnot, M. (1982) Male hegemony, social class and women's education. *Journal of Education*, 164(1):64–89.

Arnot, M. (1992) Feminism, education and the New Right, in M. Arnot and L. Barton (eds) *Voicing Concerns: Sociological Perspectives on Contemporary Education Reforms*. Wallingford, Oxfordshire: Triangle Books.

Ashendon, D., Connell, B., Dowsett, G. and Kessler, S. (1987) Teachers and working-class schooling, in D.W. Livingstone (ed.) *Critical Pedagogy and Cultural Power*. Boston, MA: Bergin and Garvey.

Asher, S.R. and Gottman, J.M. (1981) *The Development of Children's Friendships*. Cambridge: Cambridge University Press.

Atwood, M. (1990) *Cat's Eye*. London: Virago.

Bakhtin, M.M. (1981) *The Dialogic Imagination: Four Essays by M.M. Bakhtin*. Austin, TX: University of Texas Press.

Ball, S.J. (1990) *Politics and Policy Making in Education: Explorations in Policy Sociology*. London: Routledge.

Ball, S.J. (1994) Some reflections on policy theory; a brief response to Hatcher and Troyna. *Journal of Education Policy*, 9(2):171–82.

Barker, M. (1989) *Comics, Ideology, Power and the Critics*. Manchester: Manchester University Press.

Bhabba, H. (1990) The third space, in J. Rutherford (ed.) *Identity, Community, Culture, Difference*. London: Lawrence and Wishart.

Bowe, R., Ball, S.J. with Gold, A. (1992) *Reforming Education and Changing Schools: Case Studies in Policy Sociology*. London: Routledge.

Brannen, J., Dodd, K. and Oakley, A. (1991) Getting involved: the effects of research on participants. Paper presented at BSA Conference Health and Society, University of Manchester, 25–28 March.

Brown, L.M. (1994) Standing in the crossfire: a response to Tavris, Gremmen, Lykes, Davis and Contratto. *Feminism and Psychology*, 4(3):382–98.

Brown, L.M. and Gilligan, C. (1992) *Meeting at the Crossroads: Women's Psychology and Girls' Development*. Cambridge, MA: Harvard University Press.

Brunsdon, C. (1978) It is well known that by nature women are inclined to be rather personal, in Women's Studies Group (ed.) *Women Take Issue: Aspects of Women's Subordination*. London: Hutchinson in association with the Centre for Contemporary Cultural Studies (CCCS), University of Birmingham.

Bush, D. and Simmons, R. (1987) Gender and coping with the entry into early adolescence, in R.C. Barnett and G.K. Baruch (eds) *Gender and Stress*. New York: The Free Press.

Camitta, M. (1993) Vernacular writing: varieties of literacy among Philadelphia high school students, in B.V. Street (ed.) *Discourse, Ideology, and Context: Essays in the Anthropology of Literacy*. Cambridge: Cambridge University Press.

Campbell, A. (1993) *Out of Control: Men, Women and Aggression*. London: Pandora.

Canaan, J. (1986) Sleazy slang: Functions of bodily dirt in American middle class teenage slang. Paper presented at the BSA conference, The Sociology of the Life Cycle, Loughborough, 24–27 March.

Chodorow, N. (1978) *The Reproduction of Mothering: Psychoanalysis and the Sociology of Gender*. Berkeley, CA: University of California Press.

Christian-Smith, L.K. (1993a) Constituting and reconstituting desire: fiction, fantasy and femininity, in L.K. Christian-Smith (ed.) *Texts of Desire: Essays on Fiction, Femininity and Schooling*. London: Falmer Press.

Christian-Smith, L.K. (1993b) *Texts of Desire: Essays on Fiction, Femininity and Schooling*. London: Falmer Press.

Clarke, G. (1982) Defending ski jumpers: a critique of theories of youth subcultures. CCCS Occasional Paper, SP 71. Birmingham: CCCS.

Clarke, J. (1980) The skinheads and the magical recovery of community, in S. Hall and T. Jefferson (eds) *Resistance Through Rituals: Youth Subculture in Post-war Britain*. London: Hutchinson.

Clarricoates, K. (1987) Dinosaurs in the classroom – the 'hidden' curriculum in primary schools, in M. Arnot and G. Weiner (eds) *Gender and the Politics of Schooling*. London: Hutchinson for Open University Press.

Coates, J. (1996) *The Talk of Women*. Oxford: Blackwell.

Cock, J. (1980) *Maids and Madams*. Johannesburg: Ravan Press.

Cockburn, C. (1986): Women's own culture, a review of *Losing Out: Sexuality and Adolescent Girls* by Sue Lees. *Marxism Today*, 30(9):56.

Cockburn, C.K. (1987) *Two-track Training: Sex Inequalities and the YTS*. London: Macmillan.

Colman, M. (1982) *Continuous Excursions: Politics and Personal Life*. London: Pluto Press.

Connell, R.W. (1987) *Gender and Power: Society, the Person and Sexual Politics*. Cambridge: Polity Press.

Connell, R.W. (1995) *Masculinities*. Cambridge: Polity Press.

Conrad, J. (1960) *The Heart of Darkness*. New York: Bantam Books Inc.

Contratto, S. (1994) A too hasty marriage; Gilligan's developmental theory and its application to feminist clinical practice. *Feminism and Psychology*, 4(3):367–77.

Corrigan, P. (1987) In/forming schooling, in D.W. Livingstone (ed.) *Critical Pedagogy and Cultural Power*. Boston, MA: Bergin and Garvey.

Corrigan, P.D.R. (1988) The making of the boy: meditations on what grammar school did with, to, and for my body. *Journal of Education*, 170(3):142–61.

Corsaro, W. (1984) *Friendships and Culture in the Early Years*. Norwood, NY: Ablex.

Coward, R. (1984) *Female Desire*. London: Paladin.

Coward, R. (1986) The company she chooses, *The Guardian*, 20 May.

Cullingford, C. (1991) *The Inner World of the School: Children's Ideas about School*. London: Cassell.

Cunnison, S. (1989) Gender joking in the staffroom, in S. Acker (ed.) *Teachers, Gender and Careers*. London: Falmer Press.

David, M.E. (1993) *Parents, Gender and Education Reform*. Cambridge: Polity Press.

Davies, B. (1984) Friends and fights, in M. Hammersley and P. Woods (eds) *Life In School: The Sociology of Pupil Culture*. Milton Keynes: Open University Press.

Davies, B. (1989) *Frogs and Snails and Feminist Tales: Preschool Children and Gender*. Boston, MA: Allen and Unwin.

Davies, B. (1993) Beyond dualism and towards multiple subjectivities, in L.K. Christian-Smith (ed.) *Texts of Desire: Essays on Fiction, Femininity and Schooling*, London: Falmer Press.

Davies, L. (1979) Deadlier than the male?: girls' conformity and deviance in schools, in L. Barton and R. Meighan (eds) *Schools, Pupils and Deviance*. Driffield: Nafferton Books.

Davis, K. (1994) What's in a voice? methods and metaphors. *Feminism and Psychology*, 4(3):353–61.

Delamont, S. (1993) Review of *Making Connections: the Relational World of Adolescent Girls at Emma Willard School. Gender and Education*, 5(1):104–6.

Donald, J. (1985) Troublesome texts: on subjectivity and schooling. *British Journal of the Sociology of Education*, 6(3):341–51.

Douvan, E. and Adelson, J. (1966) *The Adolescent Experience*. New York: Wiley.

Eagleton, T. (1985/6) The subject of literature. *Cultural Critique*, 2:95–104.

Edelman, M. (1971) *Politics as Symbolic Action: Mass Arousal and Quiesence*. Chicago, IL: Markham.

Editorial Group (eds) (1994) *Feminism and Psychology* Special Feature 'Critical Connections: the Harvard Project on Women's Psychology and Girls' Development'.

Edwards, R. (1990) Connecting method and epistemology: a white woman Interviewing black women. *Women's Studies Internationl Forum*, 13(5):477–90.

Elias, N. (1978) *The Civilising Process*. Oxford: Basil Blackwell.

Emmerson, M.L. (1993) 'Girls' best friends: towards a study', unpublished MA thesis, Institute of Education, University of London.

Ennew, J. (1994) Time for children or time for adults? in J. Qvortrup, M. Bardy, G. Sgritta and H. Wintersberger (eds) *Childhood Matters: Social Theory, Practice and Politics*. Aldershot: European Centre Vienna/Avebury.

Epstein, D. (1993) *Changing Classroom Cultures: Anti-racism, Politics and Schools*. Stoke on Trent: Trentham Books.

Epstein, D. (1995) Out in the classroom: making sense of lesbian and gay experiences in English schools. Paper presented at Conference on New Sexual Agendas: Medical, Social and Political, Middlesex University, 14–15 July.

Epstein, J.L. and Karweit, N. (1983) *Friends in School: Patterns of Selection and Influence*. New York: Academic Press.

Evans, M. (1991) *A Good School: Life at a Girls' Grammar School in the 1950s*. London: The Women's Press.

Everhart, R.B. (1983) *Reading, Writing and Resistance: Adolescence and Labor in a Junior High School*. Boston, MA: Routledge and Kegan Paul.

Faderman, L. (1981) *Surpassing the Love of Men*. London: Junction Books.

Finch, J. (1984) 'It's great to have someone to talk to': the ethics and politics of interviewing women, in C. Bell and H. Roberts (eds) *Social Researching: Politics, Problems, Practice*. London: Routledge and Kegan Paul.

Foucault, M. (1977) *Discipline and Punish: The Birth of the Prison*. New York: Pantheon Books.

Foucault, M. (1980) *Power/Knowledge: Selected Interviews and Other Writings 1972–77*. C. Gordon (ed.) Brighton: Harvester Wheatsheaf.

Franklin, S., Lury, C. and Stacey, J. (1991) Feminism and cultural studies: pasts, presents and futures, in P. Scannell, P. Sclesinger and C. Sparks (eds) *Culture and Power: Media, Culture and Society Reader*. London: Sage.

Frazer, E. (1988) Teenage girls talking about class. *Sociology*, 22(3):343–58.

Frazer, E. and Cameron, D. (1989) Knowing what to say: the construction of gender in linguistic practice, in R. Grillo (ed.) *Social Anthropology and the Politics of Language*. London: Routledge.

Frith, S. (1981) *The Sociology of Rock*. London: Constable.

Furlong, V. (1976) Interaction sets in the classroom, in M. Stubbs and S. Delamont (eds) *Explorations in Classroom Observation*. Chichester: John Wiley and Sons.

Gallop, J. (1988) *Thinking Through the Body*. New York: Columbia University Press.

Gaskell, J. (1992) *Gender Matters from School to Work*. Milton Keynes: Open University Press.

Giddens, A. (1985) Time, space and regionalisation, in D. Gregory and J. Urry (eds) *Social Relations and Spatial Structures*. London: Macmillan.

Giddens, A. (1993) *The Transformation of Intimacy: Sexuality, Love and Eroticism in Modern Societies*. Cambridge: Polity Press.

Gilbert, P. (1993) Dolly fictions: teen romance down under, in L.K. Christian-Smith (ed.) *Texts of Desire: Essays on Fiction, Femininity and Schooling*. London: Falmer Press.

Gilligan, C. (1982) *In A Different Voice*. Cambridge, MA: Harvard University Press.

Gilligan, C., Lyons, N.P. and Hanmer, T.J. (1990) *Making Connections: The Relational World of Adolescent Girls at Emma Willard School*. Cambridge, MA: Harvard University Press.

Gluckman, M. (1963) Gossip and scandal. *Current Anthropology*, 4(3):307–15.

Gordon, T. (1995) Citizenship, difference and marginality in schools: spatial and embodied aspects. Paper Given at Unesco Colloquium, Is there a Pedagogy for Girls? University of London, Institute of Education, 10–12 January.

Gore, J. (1995) On the continuity of power relations in pedagogy. Paper presented at the International Sociology of Education conference in Sheffield, January.

Gotfrit, L. (1988) Women dancing back: disruption and the politics of pleasure. *Journal of Education*, 170(3):122–41.

Gramsci, A. (1971) *Selections from the Prison Notebook*. London: Lawrence and Wishart.

Gremmen, I. (1994) Struggling at the crossroads. *Feminism and Psychology*, 4(3): 362–6.

Griffin, C. (1982) 'The good, the bad and the ugly': images of young women in the labour market. CCCS SP 70, stencilled paper, University of Birmingham.

Griffin, C. (1985) *Typical Girls? Young Women from School to the Job Market*. London: Routledge and Kegan Paul.

Griffin, C. (1994) Absences that matter: constructions of sexuality in studies of young women's friendship groups. Paper presented at the BSA annual conference, Sexualities in Social Context, University of Central Lancashire, 28–31 March.

Griffin, C. (1995) Absences that matter: constructions of sexuality in studies of young women's friendship groups. Paper presented at the Celebrating Women's Friendship Conference, Alcuin College, University of York, 8 April.

Griffiths, V. (1995) *Adolescent Girls and their Friends: A Feminist Ethnography*. Aldershot: Avebury.

Hall, S. (1990) Cultural identity and the diaspora, in J. Rutherford (ed.) *Identity, Community, Culture and Difference*. London: Lawrence and Wishart.

Hall, S. (1991) The local and the global: globalization and ethnicity, in A. King (ed.) *Culture, Globalization and the World-System*. London: Macmillan.

Hall, S. (1992) Race, culture and communications: looking backward and forward at cultural studies. *Rethinking Marxism*, 5:10–18.

Hall, S. and Jefferson, T. (1980) *Resistance through Rituals: Youth Subcultures in Postwar Britain*. London: Hutchinson in association with CCCS.

Hargreaves, A. and Reynolds, D. (1989) Decomprehensivization, in A. Hargreaves and D. Reynolds (eds) *Education Policies: Controversies and Critiques*. London: Falmer Press.

Hasan, R. (1986) The ontogenesis of ideology: an interpretation of mother–child talk, in T. Threadgold, E.A. Grosz, G. Kress and M.A.K. Halliday (eds) *Semiotics, Ideology, Language*. Sydney: Studies in Society and Culture no. 3.

Haste, H. (1993) *The Sexual Metaphor*. Hemel Hempstead: Harvester Wheatsheaf.

Hebdige, D. (1979) *Subculture: The Meaning of Style*. London: Methuen.

Hebdige, D. (1980) The meaning of mod, in S. Hall and T. Jefferson (eds) *Resistance Through Rituals: Youth Subculture in Post-war Britain*. London: Hutchinson.

Henry, J. (1966) *Culture Against Man*. London: Tavistock.

Hewitt, R. (1986) *White Talk, Black Talk: Inter-racial Friendship and Communication Amongst Adolescents*. Cambridge: Cambridge University Press.

Hewitt, R. (1993) *Sagaland: Youth Culture Racism and Education*. Report commissioned by the Central Race Equality Unit, London, Borough of Greenwich.

Hey, V. (1983) *The Necessity of Romance*. Women's Studies Occasional Papers No. 3, University of Kent, Canterbury, available from UKC library.

Hey, V. (1988) '"The company she keeps" the social and interpersonal construction of girls' same sex friendships', unpublished PhD thesis, University of Kent, Canterbury.

Hey, V. (1994) The observation of infinite change: ethnographic evidence of girls' friendships. Paper presented at BSA Sexualities in Social Context Conference, University of Central Lancashire, Preston, 28–31 March.

Hey, V. (1995a) 'Bitching' and 'little bits of garbage': situating ethnographic evidence of girls' friendships. Paper presented at Celebrating Women's Friendship Conference, Alcuin College, University of York, 8 April.

Hey, V. (1995b) 'Bitching' and 'little bits of garbage': re-situating ethnographic evidence of girls' friendships. Revised paper from a presentation given at CREG seminar University of London, Institute of Education, 7 June.

Hey, V. (1995c) 'A game of two halves': complicities and simplicities in the debate between Right and Left about education markets: notes towards a feminist agenda. Paper presented at one-day seminar organized by CREG 'Shopping for Ideas', Feminist Analyses of Education Marketisation, Institute of Education, University of London, 20 September.

Hill, J. and Lynch, M.E. (1983) The intensification of gender-related role expectations during early adolescence, in J. Brookes-Gunn and A. Petersen (eds) *Girls at Puberty: Biological and Psychosocial Perspectives*. New York: Plenum.

Holland, J. (1993) *Sexuality and Ethnicity: Variations in Young Women's Sexual Knowledge and Practice*. London: Tufnell Press.

Holland, J. (1995) Proposal for Nuffield Research Fellowship, Social Science Research Unit, University of London Institute of Education.

Holland, J. and Ramazanoglu, C. (1994) Coming to conclusions: power and interpretation in researching young women's sexuality, in M. Maynard and J. Purvis (eds) *Researching Women's Lives from a Feminist Perspective*. London: Taylor and Francis.

Holland, J., Ramazanoglu, C., Scott, S. and Thomson, R. (1990) *'Don't Die of Ignorance, I Nearly Died of Embarrassment': Condoms in Context*. London: Tufnell Press.

Holland, J., Ramazanoglu, C., Sharpe, S. and Thomson, R. (1991) *Pressured Pleasure: Young Women and the Negotiation of Sexual Boundaries*. London: Tufnell Press.

Holland, J., Ramanzanoglu, C. and Sharpe, S. (1993) *Wimp or Gladiator: Contradictions in Acquiring Masculine Sexuality*. London: Tufnell Press.

Hollway, W. (1984) Gender difference and the production of subjectivity, in J. Henriques, W. Hollway, C. Urwin, C. Venn and V. Walkerdine (eds) *Changing the Subject: Psychology, Social Regulation and Subjectivity*. London: Methuen.

hooks, b. (1992) *Black Looks: Race and Representation*. London: Turnaround.

Horowitz, R. (1983) *Honor and the American Dream: Culture and Identity in a Chicago Community*. New Brunswick, NJ: Rutgers University Press.

Hudson, B. (1984) Femininity and adolescence, in A. McRobbie and M. Nava (eds) *Gender and Generation*. Basingstoke: Macmillan.

Jackson, S. (1995) Heterosexuality as a problem for feminist theory, in M. Maynard and J. Purvis (eds) *(Hetero)Sexual Politics*. London: Falmer Press.

James, H. (1987) *Portrait of a Lady*. Harmondsworth, Middlesex: Penguin Books.

Johnson, F. and Aries, E. (1983a) Conversational patterns among same-sex pairs of late adolescent close friends. *Journal of Genetic Psychology*, 142:225–38.

Johnson, F. and Aries, E. (1983b) The talk of women friends. *Women's Studies International Forum*, 6(4):353–61.

Johnson, R. (1979) 'Really useful knowledge': radical education and working-class culture 1790–1848, in J. Clarke, C. Critcher and R. Johnson (eds) *Working*

Class Culture: Studies in History and Theory. London: Hutchinson University Library in association with the Centre for Contemporary Cultural Studies (CCCS) University of Birmingham.

Johnson, R. (1986) The story so far: and further transformations? in D. Punter (ed.) *Introduction to Contemporary Cultural Studies*. London: Longman.

Jones, A. (1988) Which girls are 'learning to lose?': gender, class, race and talking in the classroom, in S. Middleton (ed.) *Women and Education in Aotearoa*. Wellington: Allen and Unwin.

Jones, A. (1993) Becoming a 'girl': post-structuralist suggestions for educational research. *Gender and Education*, 5(2):157–66.

Jones, D. (1980) Gossip: notes on women's oral culture. *Women's Studies International Quarterly*, 3:193–8.

Kennedy, R. (1986) Women's friendships on Crete: a psychological perspective, in J. Dubisch (ed.) *Gender and Power in Rural Greece*. Princeton, NJ: Princeton University Press.

Kenway, J. and Blackmore, J. (1995) Pleasure and pain: beyond feminist authoritarianism and therapy in the curriculum. Paper presented at the Unesco Colloquium, 'Is there a Pedagogy for Girls?' Institute of Education, University of London, 10–12 January.

Kuhn, A. (1995) *Family Secrets: Acts of Memory and Imagination*. London: Verso.

Lambart, A. (1976) The sisterhood, in M. Hammersley and P. Woods (eds) *The Process of Schooling: A Sociological Reader*. London: Routledge and Kegan Paul in association with Open University Press.

Lauretis de, T. (1984) *Alice Doesn't*. Bloomington, IN: Indiana University Press.

Leeds Revolutionary Feminists (1981) 'Political lesbianism': the case against heterosexuality, in *Love Your Enemy? The Debate Between Heterosexual Feminism and Political Lesbianism*. London: OnlyWoman Press.

Lees, S. (1986) *Losing Out: Sexuality and Adolescent Girls*. London: Hutchinson.

Leonard, D. (1980) *Sex and Generation: A Study of Courtship and Weddings*. London: Tavistock.

Lever, J. (1976) Sex differences in the games children play. *Social Problems*, 23:478–87.

Llewellyn, M. (1980) Studying girls at school: the implications of confusion, in R. Deem (ed.) *Schooling for Women's Work*. London: Routledge and Kegan Paul.

Lykes, M.B. (1994) Whose meeting at which crossroads? a response to Brown and Gilligan. *Feminism and Psychology*, 4(3):345–9.

Mac an Ghaill, M. (1988) *Young, gifted and black: student–teacher relations in the schooling of black youth*. Milton Keynes: Open University Press.

Mac an Ghaill, M. (1994) *The Making of Men: Masculinities, Sexualities and Schooling*. Buckingham: Open University Press.

McRobbie, A. (1978) Working class girls and the culture of femininity, in Women's Studies Group (ed.) *Women Take Issue: Aspects of Women's Subordination*. London: Hutchinson.

McRobbie, A. (1980) 'Settling accounts with subcultures': a feminist critique. *Screen Education*, 34:37–49.

McRobbie, A. (1982a) *Jackie*: an ideology of adolescent femininity, in B. Waites, T. Bennett and G. Martin (eds) *Popular Culture: Past and Present*. London: Croom Helm and Open University Press.

McRobbie, A. (1982b) The politics of feminist research: between talk, text and action. *Feminist Review*, 12:46–57.

McRobbie, A. (1991) *Feminism and Youth Culture: From* Jackie *to* Just Seventeen. London: Macmillan.

McRobbie, A. and Garber, J. (1980) Girls and subcultures, in S. Hall and T. Jefferson (eds) *Resistance Through Rituals: Youth Subcultures in Post-war Britain*. London: Hutchinson.

McRobbie, A. and McCabe, T. (1981) *Feminism for Girls: An Adventure Story*. London: Routledge and Kegan Paul.

Mahony, P. (1985) *Schools for the Boys? Co-education Reassessed*. London: Hutchinson.

Mandell, N. (1991) The least-adult role in studying children, in F.C. Waksler (ed.) *Studying the Social Worlds of Children: Sociological Readings*. London: Falmer Press.

Measor, L. (1985) Interviewing: a strategy in qualitative research, in R.G. Burges (ed.) *Strategies of Educational Research: Qualitative Methods*. London: Falmer Press.

Meyenn, R.J. (1980) School girls' peer groups, in P. Woods (ed.) *Pupil Strategies*. London: Croom Helm.

Miles, M.B. and Huberman, A.M. (1984) *Qualitative Data Analysis: A Sourcebook of New Methods*. Beverly Hills, CA: Sage Publications.

Miller, J. (1990) *Seductions: Studies in Reading and Culture*. London: Virago.

Miller, J. (1991) Some of our best friends: review of McRobbie, A. (1991) and Walkerdine, V. (1990). *New Statesman and Society*, 1 February.

Milroy, L. (1987) *Language and Social Networks*. London: Routledge.

Minolin, A. (1986) Secret women's writing. *Spare Rib*, 168, July: 49.

Mirza, H.S. (1992) *Young, Female and Black*. London: Routledge.

Modleski, T. (1982) *Loving with a Vengeance*. New York: Methuen.

Morgan, D.L. (1990) Combining the strengths of social networks, social support and personal relationships, in S. Duck and R.S. Silver (eds) *Personal Relationships and Social Support*. London: Sage.

Morrow, V. (1993) 'Rarely seen and never heard': Methodological and ethical considerations of researching children. Paper given at BSA Conference, Research Imaginations, University of Essex, 5–8 April.

Nelsen, R.W. (1987) Books, boredom and behind bars: an explanation of apathy and hostility in our schools, in T. Wotherspoon (ed.) *The Political Economy of Canadian Schooling*. Toronto: Methuen.

Nilan, P. (1991) Exclusion, inclusion and moral ordering in two girls' friendship groups. *Gender and Education*, 3(1):163–82.

Oakley, A. (1974) *Housewife*. London: Allen Lane.

Oakley, A. (1981) Interviewing women: a contradiction in terms, in H. Roberts (ed.) *Doing Feminist Research*. London: Routledge and Kegan Paul.

O'Brien, M. (1987) Education and patriarchy, in D.W. Livingstone (ed.) *Critical Pedagogy and Cultural Power*. Boston, MA: Bergin and Garvey.

O'Connor, P. (1992) *Friendships Between Women: A Critical Review*. Hemel Hempstead: Harvester Wheatsheaf.

Opie, A. (1992) Qualitative research, appropriation of the 'other' and empowerment. *Feminist Review*, 40, Spring: 52–69.

Opie, P. and Opie, I. (1959) *The Lore and Language of School Children*. Oxford: Oxford University Press.

Orbach, S. (1986) *Fat is a Feminist Issue*. London: Arrow.

Patai, D. (1994) When method becomes power, in A. Gitlin (ed.) *Power and Method*. New York: Routledge.

Patton, M.Q. (1990) *Qualitative Evaluation and Research Methods*. London: Sage.

Payne, I. (1980) A working-class girl in a grammar school, in D. Spender and E. Sarah (eds) *Learning to Lose: Sexism and Education*. London: The Women's Press.

Pollard, A. (1984) Goodies, jokers and gangs, in M. Hammersley and P. Woods (eds) *Life in the school: the sociology of pupil culture*. Milton Keynes: Open University Press.

Prendergast, S. and Prout, A. (1980) What will I do . . . ? teenage girls and the construction of motherhood. *Sociological Review*, 28:517–36.

Prout, A. and James, A. (1990) A new paradigm for the sociology of childhood? provenance, promise and problems, in A. James and A. Prout (eds) *Constructing and Reconstructing Childhood: Contemporary Issues in the Sociological Study of Childhood*. London: Falmer Press.

Raymond, J. (1986) *A Passion for Friends: Towards a Philosophy of Female Affection*. London: The Women's Press.

Reinharz, S. (1992) *Feminist Methods in Social Research*. New York: Oxford University Press.

Remmington, P. (1983) Women in the police: integration or separation. *Qualitative Sociology*, 6:118–35.

Ribbens, J. and Edwards, R. (1995) Introducing qualitative research on women in families and households. *Women's Studies International Forum*, 18(3):247–58.

Rich, A. (1979) *On Lies, Secrets, and Silence*. Toronto: W.W. Norton and Company.

Rich, A. (1980) Compulsory heterosexuality and lesbian existence. *Signs: Journal of Women in Culture and Society*, 5(4):631–60.

Richards, C. (1990) Intervening in popular pleasures: media studies and the politics of subjectivity, in D. Buckingham (ed.) *Watching Media Learning: Making Sense of Media Education*. London: Falmer Press.

Richards, C. (forthcoming) *Youth, Identity and Difference in Media Education*. London: Taylor and Francis.

Riddell, S. (1989) Pupils, resistance and gender codes. *Gender and Education*, 1(2):183–97.

Riviere, J. (1985) Womanliness as masquerade, in V. Burgin, J. Donald and C. Kaplan (eds) *Formations of Fantasy*. London: Methuen.

Roland Martin, J. (1995) A girls' pedagogy 'in relationship'. Paper presented at the Unesco Colloquium, Is there a Pedagogy for Girls? University of London, Institute of Education, 10–12 January.

Rossiter, A.B. (1994) Chips, Coke and rock 'n' roll: mediation of an invitation to a first dance party. *Feminist Review*, 46, Spring: 1–20.

Rowbotham, S. (1973) *Woman's Consciousness, Man's World*. London: Penguin.

Rubin, G. (1975) The traffic in women notes on the political economy of sex, in R. Reiter (ed.) *Towards an Anthropology for Women*. New York: Monthly Review Press.

Rubin, Z. (1980) *Children's Friendships: The Developing Child*. London: Open Books.

Ruddick, S. (1990) *Maternal Thinking: Towards a Politics of Peace*. London: The Women's Press.

Rutherford, J. (1990) A place called home: Identity and the cultural politics of difference, in J. Rutherford (ed.) *Identity: Community, Culture, Difference*. London: Lawrence and Wishart.

Sartre, J.P. (1963) *Saint Genet*. London: WH Allen.

Scheurich, J. (1995) A postmodernist critique of research interviewing. *International Journal of Qualitative Studies in Education*, 6(3):239–52.

Segal, L. (1987) *Is the Future Female?* London: Virago.

Segal, L. (1990) *Slow Motion: Changing Masculinities*. London: Virago.

Sherratt, N. (1983) Girls, jobs and glamour. *Feminist Review*, 15:47–60.

Side, K. (1995) Making and breaking women's friendships in feminist theory. Paper given at the Celebrating Women's Friendship Conference, Alcuin College, University of York, 8 April.

Simmons, R. and Blyth, D.A. (1987) *Moving into Adolescence: The Impact of Pubertal Change and School Context*. Hawthorne, NY: Aldine de Gruyter.

Skeggs, B. (1991) Review essay: postmodernism: what is all the fuss about? *British Journal of the Sociology of Education*, 12(2):255–67.

Skeggs, B. (1994) Situating the production of feminist ethnography, in M. Maynard and J. Purvis (eds) *Researching Women's Lives from a Feminist Perspective*. London: Taylor and Francis.

Smilansky, M. (1991) *Friendship in Adolescence and Young People*. Gaithersburg, MD: Psychosocial and Education Publications.

Smith, D.E. (1988) Femininity as discourse, in L.G. Roman, L.K. Christian-Smith, and E. Ellsworth (eds) *Becoming Feminine: The Politics of Popular Culture*. London: Falmer Press.

Smith-Rosenberg, C. (1975) The female world of love and ritual: relations between women in nineteenth century America. *Signs: Journal of Women in Culture and Society*, 1(1):1–29.

Solberg, A. (1992) The social construction of childhood: children's contributions. Paper given at Childhood Study Group seminar, Social Science Research Unit, Institute of Education, London, 3 June.

Spender, D. and Sarah, E. (1980) *Learning to Lose: Sexism and Education*. London: Women's Press.

Stacey, J. (1988) Can there be a feminist ethnography? *Women's Studies International Forum*, 11(1):21–7.

Stacey, J. (1990) On resistance, ambivalence and feminist theory: a response to Carol Gilligan. *Michigan Quarterly Review Special Issue*, 24(4):537–46.

Stanworth, M. (1981) *Gender and Schooling: A Study of Sexual Divisions in the Classroom*. Pamphlet No. 7, London: WRRC.

Steedman, C. (1982) *The Tidy House: Little Girls Writing*. London: Virago.

Steedman, C. (1985) Prisonhouses. *Feminist Review*, 20, Summer: 7–21.

Steedman, C. (1986) *Landscape for a Good Woman: A Story of Two Lives*. London: Virago.

Steedman, C. (1992) *Past Tenses: Essays on Writing Autobiography and History*. London: Rivers Oram Press.

Taylor, S. (1993) Transforming the texts: towards a feminist classroom practice, in L.K. Christian-Smith (ed.) *Texts of Desire: Essays on Fiction, Femininity and Schooling*. London: Falmer Press.

Thorne, B. (1993) *Gender Play: Girls and Boys in School*. Buckingham: Open University Press.

Urwin, C. (1985) Constructing motherhood: the persuasion of normal development, in C. Steedman, C. Urwin and V. Walkerdine (eds) *Language, Gender and Childhood*, London: Routledge and Kegan Paul.

Van Maanen, J. (1988) *Tales of the Field: On Writing Ethnography*. Chicago, IL: University of Chicago Press.

Vik Kleven, K. (1993a) Girl culture as a chastity belt. *Nordic Journal of Women's Studies*, 2:90–104.

Vik Kleven, K. (1993b) In deadly earnest or postmodern irony: new gender clashes? *Nordic Journal of Youth Research*, 1(4):40–59.

Voloshinov, V.N. (1973) *Marxism and the Philosophy of Language*, trans. L. Matejka and I.R. Titunik. New York: Seminar Press.

Walkerdine, V. (1981) Sex, power and pedagogy. *Screen Education*, 38:1–24.

Walkerdine, V. (1984) Some day my prince will come: young girls and the preparation for adolescent sexuality, in A. McRobbie and M. Nava (eds) *Gender and Generation*. London: Macmillan.

Walkerdine, V. (1985) On the regulation of speaking and silence, in C. Steedman, C. Urwin and V. Walkerdine (eds) *Language, Gender and Childhood*. London: Routledge and Kegan Paul.

Walkerdine, V. (1986) Post-structuralist theory and everyday social practices: the family and the school, in S. Wilkinson (ed.) *Feminist Social Psychology: Developing Theory and Practice*. Milton Keynes: Open University Press.

Walkerdine, V. (1987) Femininity as performance. *Oxford Review of Education*, 15 (3):267–79.

Walkerdine, V. (1990) *Schoolgirl Fictions*. London: Verso.

Walkerdine, V. and Lucey, H. (1989) *Democracy in the Kitchen: Regulating Mothers and Socialising Daughters*. London: Virago.

Warren, C.B. (1988) *Gender Issues in Field Research*. Newbury Park, CA: Sage Publications.

Weiner, A.B. (1976) *Women of Value, Men of Reknown: New Perspectives in Trobriand Exchange*. Austin, TX: University of Texas: Press.

Wertsch, J.V. (1991) *Voices of the Mind: A Sociocultural Appraoch to Mediated Action*. London: Harvester Wheatsheaf.

Wexler, P. (1992) *Becoming Somebody: Toward a Social Psychology of School*. London: Falmer Press.

White, P. (1990) Friendship and education. *Journal of the Philosophy of Education*, 24(1):81–91.

Whitehead, A. (1976) Sexual antagonism in Herefordshire, in. D. Barker and S. Allen (eds) *Dependence and Exploitation in Work and Marriage*. London: Longman.

Williams, L. (1988) A jury of their peers: Marlene Gorris's *A Question of Silence*, in E.A. Kaplan (ed.) *Postmodernism and its Discontents: Theories, Practices*. London: Verso.

Williams, R. (1989) Resources of hope, in R. Gable (ed.) *Resources of Hope*. London: Verso.

Williamson, J. (1981/2) How does girl number twenty understand ideology? *Screen Education*, 40, Autumn–Winter: 80–7.

Williamson, J. (1986) A piece of the action: images of 'woman' in the photography of Cindy Sherman, in J. Williamson (ed.) *Consuming Passions: The Dynamics of Popular Culture*. London: Marion Boyars.

Willis, P. (1977) *Learning to Labour: How Working Class Kids Get Working Class Jobs.* London: Gower.

Wilson, E. (1983) All the Rage. *New Socialist*, 14, November/December: 22–6.

Wilton, T. (1993) Queer subjects: lesbians, heterosexual women and the academy, in M. Kennedy, C. Lubelska and V. Walsh (eds) *Making Connections: Women's Studies; Women's Movements; Women's Lives*, London: Taylor and Francis.

Wittig, M. (1973) *Les Guerilleres*. New York: Avon Books.

Wolpe, A.M. (1988) 'Experience' as analytical framework: does it account for girls' education? in M. Cole (ed.) *Bowles and Gintis Revisited: Correspondence and Contradiction in Educational Theory*. London: Falmer Press.

Wolpe, A.M. (1989) *Within School Walls*. London: Routledge.

Woods, P. (1977) 'Having a laugh': an antidote to schooling, in P. Woods (ed.) *Open University Block 2 The Process of Schooling*. Milton Keynes: Open University.

Woods, P. (1983) *Sociology and the School: An Interactionist Viewpoint*. London: Routledge and Kegan Paul.

Wulff, H. (1988) 'Twenty girls: growing up, ethnicity and excitement in a South London microculture', unpublished doctoral dissertation, Department of Social Anthropology, University of Stockholm.

Index

CHILDREN, HEALTH AND THE SOCIAL ORDER

Berry Mayall

Children's health is usually studied in relation to health services, and their learning within the school service; and traditionally children are perceived as the objects of these services. Yet health experience crosses institutional settings, and takes place at home too. And children have their own views on health maintenance and are active in the project of their own lives.

This book reverses traditional approaches and considers children's views on health care and their experiences of the home and school as sites for health maintenance, restoration and promotion.

* How do adult understandings of children and childhood serve to structure the childhoods children live?
* How do sociological insights like feminism and the sociology of the body help in the task of siting children within sociology?

Children, Health and the Social Order draws on a number of studies carried out by the author, and in particular on a study in one primary school of children's, parents' and school staff's understandings of child health maintenance and care.

The study of children as a social group provides a wider sociological context of the book which explores, using feminist insights, the construction of knowledge, body–mind links and the division of labour. It will be of interest to professionals in child health and education as well as students of sociology, anthropology, education and health.

Contents

Introduction – The politics of child health – Constructions of childhood – Home and school as children's social environments – Children's lived bodies in everyday life – Adult time, children's time – Children and childhoods revisited – Bibliography – Index.

192pp   0 335 19282 3 (Paperback)   0 335 19283 1 (Hardback)